D0661210

**WHAT HAPPENS IN THIS HOUSE 2: THE
FATHER & SON
Written By-
ALEIA LATAY**

**Copyright © 2016 by True Glory Publications
Published by True Glory Publications
Join our Mailing List by texting True Glory to 99000
or click here http://optin.mobiniti.com/V2Yr**

Facebook:

*This novel is a work of fiction. Any resemblances to
actual events, real people, living or dead, organizations,
establishments or locales are products of the author's
imagination. Other names, characters, places, and
incidents are used fictitiously.*

Cover Design: Tina Louise
Editor: Shanay McKiver

*All rights reserved. No part of this book may be used or
reproduced in any form or by any means electronic or
mechanical, including photocopying, recording or by
information storage and retrieval system, without the
written permission from the publisher and writer.
Because of the dynamic nature of the Internet, and Web
addresses or links contained in this book may have
changed since publication, and may no longer be valid.
The views expressed in this work are solely those of the
author and do not necessarily reflect the views of the
publisher and the publisher hereby disclaims any
responsibility for them.*

Table of Contents

ATLANTIC CITY FREE PUBLIC LIBRARY

DEDICATION

The Late Great Hustella Smith

A Special Thanks

Thanks to all the supporters, my readers and family as well as my publishing family!

SYNOPSIS

Jasmine, Jackson, and Joy have buried their father along with the dark secrets. Moving on since then, they have sold the house and all three are back in Canton, Mississippi. Some might say it was fate, Joy seems to think it was a plan all along.

When they discover the truth behind the house they grew up in. It is up to the three to face the evil head on or walk away. Joy has enough issues dealing with her son who has a child on the way. Not to mention she is getting the feel of motherhood herself.

Apart from that, Joy is torn between Nathan and Charlene. Elijah is convinced he isn't the father of Juniqua's unborn child. With Schools scouting him and his girlfriend Riley learning his new living arrangements. Elijah has enough stress to deal with for the moment.

Jackson is one second from losing his mind without his wife and kids. At a cross roads, forgiving his father isn't so easy. Losing his own family because of his daddy issues. Jackson returns to the house thinking if he forgives he could move on. After learning, what happened to his father. Jackson now understands why his father was the way he was. Seeking help from his siblings they seemed to think that he is losing it.

Jasmine is broken after learning her newly husband's dirty secret. Unsure if she will leave or stay. Jasmine focuses on the fact that she will soon be a mother herself.

Carmen returns home and runs into an old friend. When they begin to reminisce one thing leads to another. This family is put to the test with numerous obstacles thrown at them. What happened in that house left an everlasting mark on each and every one of them. Returning back in the house might be their only option to bury the darkness for good. The house is still standing filled with evil and untold stories. Are you ready see what the spirits reveal next?

Chapter One

Jackson

"I Am Not My Father"

Breaking news, a family relocating to Canton, Mississippi, purchased the home of the late Jack Johnson. The man who was brutally murdered and whose killers are awaiting trial. The new owner's grandmother says her grandson took her to see the house. What she has to say is very disturbing, here is a clip of the interview.

"That house took my grandson's soul! I seen the demon in that house its evil. Somebody has to finish what has started the demon is getting stronger." The old lady yelled.

Ignoring the news on the television, Jackson held the phone, he called Carmen a dozen times. She hadn't called or so much as to send him a text message. Grabbing his bottle of Whisky, he turned the bottle up and took a swig.

With tears in his eyes Jackson wondered if she had moved on with another man. Not that he could blame her after everything he had put her through.

"I was going to treat you better Carmen. You left me and you said we could work things out. How could you leave me with nothing!"

Jackson yelled.

Dialing her number over and over the operator said the number was no longer in service. Jackson tossed the bottle up against the wall. He was tired of sitting in his apartment alone. While Carmen was miles away doing God knows what.

"I was a fool to ever think we could work things out."

Jackson said.

Flashes of his father beating his mother caused him to hold his head. Then flashes similar of him beating Carmen flashed in his mind.

"No!"

Jackson yelled.

An image of his mother on the floor crying flashed. Then an image of Carmen on the ground in tears.

"I'm not like him!"

Jackson yelled.

The flashes were coming in back to back causing Jackson to throw anything within his reach.

"I'm not him! I'm Not my father!"

Jackson screamed.

The flashes stopped, Jackson cried he was losing it and he knew he needed help. Everything went silent as if time stood still. Jackson looked around until seeing his keys on the nearby end table.

He needed to see his therapist. His sister Joy was nice enough to pay for his sessions. She was worried about his mental state since Carmen left. Jackson had to admit he felt as if he was near a nervous breakdown. The only peace he had was when he worked. He hadn't slept good since the day of his father's funeral.

Driving himself to the therapist's office, Jackson was stopped at a red light. Flashes of a young boy getting beat was all he could see. Unsure of why these visions was coming in so vividly. Jackson closed his eyes and tried to stop the flashes.

Reopening his eyes the light changed green. Speeding off, he wasn't far from the therapist. In the parking lot Jackson thought of all the times he put his hands on his wife. It had torn his heart to imagine all that he put Carmen through.

Talking with a stranger wouldn't change a thing. What was done was done, Jackson knew he was losing it. Deciding to have himself a drink. Jackson bought a fifth of Hennessey and a pint of Paul.

Returning home, he turned on his stereo. Raising the bottle for a toast, Jackson let the words of Anthony Hamilton touch his soul. Sip after sip until he felt numb. Jackson stared at old pictures of he and Carmen when they first got together.

"What the fuck is wrong with me?"

He yelled fighting back the tears.

"Why couldn't I have just treated you better baby?"

He whispered while staring at the picture. Looking up, Jackson nearly passed out. Either his mind was playing tricks on him. Or he had just seen his father standing in the doorway.

"Why the fuck you here now?! You didn't care, you never cared about me! Motherfucker I hate myself for being just like you!"

Jackson yelled.

The imagine of his father had long passed. Still an angry Jackson was getting it all out.

"You didn't care about momma. You didn't deserve her, you ungrateful bastard! What you did to her and Joy, even me. I will never forgive you I'm glad you're dead. Rot in hell where you belong daddy! You hear me motherfucker rot in hell!"

Jackson yelled as he threw his bottle at the wall. The room begin to spin and Jackson could barely stand. The words sorry was heard as plain as day. Jackson didn't want to hear the voices.

Leaving his apartment, he stumbled to his car. The last thing he remembered was locking himself in his car. After blacking out, Jackson went into a deep sleep.

Waking up to a neighbor tapping on his car window. Jackson tried to remember what happened. Drinking had only made his situation worst. Cleaning up himself he felt sick to his stomach. Unable to go in to work he called out.

He desperately needed to talk to someone. So, he did an emergency session with his therapist.

"Mr. Johnson, do you want to discuss this past week's events?"

The therapist asked.

"I saw my father, he was standing there. No words were said from him, just a look. I haven't heard from my kids or Carmen. Doc I feel like death is lingering near me."

Jackson spoke afraid as if he might die soon.

"What makes you think that?"

The therapist asked.

"I haven't been able to sleep or eat since my father's funeral. I keep seeing flashes of all the bad things I've done."

Jackson replied.

"Tell me about your relationship with your father. What was your last conversation like?"

She asked.

Jackson sat back on the chaise and recalled the last conversation he had with his father. It was years ago, back when Carmen had finished giving birth to his first child. Jackson would never forget that day.

It was the day he vowed to never reach out to his father again. In fact, that was the start of him abusing Carmen. It was only after reaching out to Jack.

"Looks like it's a healthy baby boy Mr. and Mrs. Johnson."
The nurse said wiping him off.

Jackson teared up while holding his firstborn child. The feeling of fatherhood was amazing. Wanting to patch things up with his own father, Jackson decided to reach out to his own.

"Baby let me call a few of my people's. Tell my sisters that my little man is here."

Jackson smiled placing their son in her arms. Carmen's family was at the hospital. Joy was on her way, so was Jasmine. Getting out his cell, Jackson dialed his father's number.

The house number had been the same for years. After a few rings, Jack finally picked up.

"Hello?"

His father answered sounding like his usual self.

"Hey pop, it's me Jackson."

Jackson said hoping to get a positive reaction out of him.

"What you want boy I ain't got no money for you."

Jack spat coldly.

"I don't need no money pop, I called to see how you was doing."

Jackson said.

"I'm alive ain't I? Then I'm doing just fine."

Jack said.

"That's good dad listen, I'm married now and my wife just gave birth to my son. I was hoping you would want us to come visit soon. That way you can see your grandson and daughter in law."

Jackson smiled.

"Ion wanna see that whore you call a wife. Or that bastard child, nobody staying in my house. You go on get your own

family a house. Be a man for once, Lord knows you was a lazy
child growing up!"
   Jack spat.
   "Lazy! Let me tell you something, you're a poor excuse of a
fucking father. What kind of man treats his family like this? You
beat my mother into an early grave. Your worthless pathetic ass
didn't even deserve her. You treated your children like shit! You
have beaten me down physically and emotionally. I figured out
why you did it too. You couldn't handle having a son with more
education than you. I have a degree and a better paying job than
you did. I'm a better husband than you were and I will be a
better father than you. I hope you rot in that house because if
anyone deserves to suffer it's you Jack! One day it's all going to
come back on you. When it does, no one will be able to help you.
Not even your precious angel Jasmine. Me and Joy have made it
this far without a father. I don't know why I even bothered
reaching out to you."
   Jackson spat.
   "That's just fine by me boy!"
   Jack yelled and Jackson hung up on him.
   He was so upset at his father he could use a drink. After all
these years, you would think he would change. That entire night
all Jackson thought about was his evil father. Growing up in that
house nearly broke him. He would never put his son through
what he went through.

   The therapist asked Jackson did he regret his last words to
his father.
   "No, he deserved to finally hear me for once. The damage he
caused in me and my sisters, we were always too afraid to speak
up. For once I did, and as a man it felt good. That night I had
nightmares of all the times my father hit my mother. I even
started to blame myself. I hated myself for not being able to save
my mother."
   Jackson said.
   "So Jackson, what made you abuse your wife?"
   She asked.
   "I take blame for my actions. Once the nightmares came, the
only thing that kept them away was when I would drink. It

started off a beer or two before bed. Graduated to a pint a whiskey every night. Then I would get so angry sometimes. It was like something or someone was inside of me. Controlling me to do those awful things. One time I remember I was laughing on the couch. Next thing I now I'm standing over Carmen strangling her. That's when I knew I had a serious problem. Sometimes I didn't even realize I was beating her. It was like an out of body experience. I'm looking at myself as I'm hitting her. I didn't have control, I wanted to stop but couldn't. It was scary, and for a month I slept on the couch. Sort of figured if I distance myself from my wife, then maybe I wouldn't be able to harm her. Nightmares came back and the cycle repeated."

Jackson said.

"Do you feel your father is the blame for your sudden uncontrollable anger episodes?"

She asked.

"He did damage me, but I do take partial blame. I just wanted to prove I could be a better man. So far I've failed at convincing myself."

He replied.

"What else do you think you could try that you haven't already tried?"

The therapist asked.

Jackson pondered on the question. He had been to AA meetings, church, you name it. The only thing he could think of was reaching out to his father.

"I never got the chance to sit down and talk to him."

Jackson replied.

"Him as in your father Mr. Johnson?"

She asked to clarify his response.

"Yes, maybe I need closure you know. Joy found letters from our father and she forgave him just like that. Like it was easy but I just can't forgive what he has done."

Jackson said.

"In my opinion Jackson, maybe you should get things out. Your sister expressed through your father's letters. Perhaps you could do something similar. Communicate to your father through something left of him."

She said.

"The only thing Jack has left is that raggedy house we sold."
He said sitting up.

"I'm sure visiting the property wouldn't be a big of a deal. Try contacting the owner and get closure Jackson. You can finally put all of this mess behind you for once and for all."
She told him.

"You're right and I will, thank you miss Roberts."
Jackson said standing to leave.

The new owner of the home had passed. Jackson had to talk to the guy who bought the house grandmother. Remembering that Joy had the contact number to reach her. He needed to check on his sisters anyway. Stopping by to visit would kill two birds with one stone.

"Sup unc, you got a minute?"
Elijah asked as Jackson walked up on the porch of his sister's home.

"Always nephew what's up with you?"
Jackson asked him while hugging him.

"It's about my coach, mom is cool with him you probably know him too. His name Nathan anyways, he kicked me off the team. Scouts coming out this weekend, you think you could talk to him for me? I think him and ma fell out or something."
Elijah said.

"Nathan and yo mom was forever falling out. They used to get on my nerves too. He and I are cool so I will give him a holla. I can't have my talented nephew on the sidelines. You gotta go pro and hook yo unc up with a Ferrari."
Jackson smiled as they slapped palms.

"I got you unc soon as I go pro."
Elijah laughed.

Jackson walked in the house and saw Joy on the couch with Jas.

"Hey my two headaches, what y'all been up to?"
Jackson said having a seat in a chair.

"Not much, what's been up with you?"
Joy asked.

"Life, I got a few things I'm working on. Starting with our father, anybody heard from the owners of the house?"
Jackson asked.

"You mean us again, them people sold us the house back."
Joy said.

"Damn, and I'm paying rent could have just stayed in the house myself."
Jackson said.

"Have it, the yard look a mess anyways."
Joy said handing him the keys to the house.

"Good cause the neighbors in my apartment building are working my nerves. I might have to move in the house tonight. Glad we didn't get rid of the furniture in the house."
Jackson said.

"Hey could you check in my old room and see if those divorce papers are still on the bed?"
Jasmine asked.

"Yeah, you talk to David lately?"
He asked.

"Yes, but he still saying the same ole bull about him being curious. And that all men go through that phase."
Jasmine replied.

"Not all men, I don't know what "in the closet" men he been hanging around with. I never went through no phase. Never have and never will he's a damn lie. Why don't he just admit that he's gay and move on."
Jackson said.

"I said the same thing, all he does is call me non-stop."
Jasmine said.

"Well, call me if he steps out of line. I will let you know if I see those papers. Love you both, think I'm gonna head over to the house and move in a few things."
Jackson said.

"Hey you hear from Carmen and the kids yet we been calling. I guess her phone is disconnected."
Joy said.

"I haven't heard a word from her. She with her people so I doubt if I'll hear from them anytime soon."
Jackson shrugged.

"Dang, that's messed up brother. Keep trying to reach out to her maybe she will come around."
Jasmine said.

Jackson nodded but his main focus was to get closure.

Driving to the house, Jackson saw that the caution tape was still on the porch. The sun was going down and Jackson had no time to start on yard work. Gathering the tape, he tossed it in the trashcan. Using the key, Jackson struggled to get the front door open.

"Damn police, I bet they the ones that fucked this door up."

Jackson spat pushing his weight onto the door.

The door flew open, and Jackson stumbled inside. Searching for the light switch, Jackson found it and turned on the lights in the living room.

The house was dead silent. Shutting the front door, which squeaked; until the door latched. The hardwood floor creaked with every step he took.

Jackson looked around the house, each room held painful memories. Searching the kitchen for something to drink out of. Jackson found an empty jar to go along with his bottle of whiskey.

Going back to his car he unloaded his stereo into the house as well. After hooking it up he played his favorite mix cd. Singer Kem's voice carried throughout the house. Sipping his drink, he sang along and danced in the middle of the living room floor.

"There would be no more lies
Somebody tell me why it feels like I'm dying.
Lord what's come over me? Oooh baby can't you see that.
I can't stop loving you, I can't help myself. And I can't get over you, No matter what I tell myself."

Jackson sang.

Spinning around, the walls paint began to look freshly painted new. The smell of fried fish hit Jackson like a ton of bricks. In a blink of an eye the house were filled with people. It was as if he were looking through a different set of eyes.

His mother entered the room handing him a beer. She looked no more than twenty. He had never seen her more beautiful.

"Jack, baby let's dance."

She smiled.

Jackson saw his parents dancing. No longer looking through another pair of eyes. Jackson was now an extra in this flashback movie. No matter how he tried to interact with others, Jackson remained invisible.

This must have been when they first moved into the house he thought. The floors shined and outside the sun shined bright and cars were lined up. Everything looked back in the day. From the hairdos to the clothes. Jack's hair was waved back like a temptation. His mother sported an up do like a young Diana Ross.

Everybody was having a good time. Jack turned when someone whispered in his ear. Rushing out of the house, Jackson wondered what was going on. Next thing you know he was inside of a hospital room. Seeing his father cry for the first time.

The lady in the hospital bed sort of favored his aunt Stella. Jackson couldn't believe what he was seeing. It was like a movie but he knew the people were real and of the past. Jackson watched as his uncle Walter walked in the room.

"Jack, now that momma gone someone is going to have to tell daddy."

Walter cried.

"To hell with him you hear me! He caused momma to suffer you remember that Walter."

Jack spat.

"He doesn't know yet someone has to tell him."

Walter said.

Jackson never met his grandparents, only heard stories of them. Jack stormed out of the hospital room. Following him, Jackson was still confused as to what was going on. Jack was at an old house not too far from their own house. On the porch sat an old man with a frown.

"What you want boy?"

The old man spat.

"She gone daddy momma passed on. No need to show your face to her funeral. You done enough helping her into an early grave."

Jack said.

"You got some nerves boy! I go on if I want to you, hear me boy?"

The old man yelled.

"Don't bother daddy, you done enough."

Jack said.

"I should have killed you a long time ago. Should of watch you take your last breath."

The old man spat.

Jack ran up the stairs of the porch grabbing the old man by the throat. It was almost as if he was asking to be hurt. The old man kept right on throwing insults towards Jack.

"You will never amount to a damn thing boy. You still live in fear from me boy! That bitch of yours won't amount to shit, neither will your kids, if you ever have any."

Jack strangled him as those hateful words escaped his father's mouth.

"I ain't afraid of you anymore you hear me?! I'm not a boy anymore you can't hurt me. You hear me old bastard? I'm not afraid!"

Jack yelled.

Jackson tried to pull his father off of the man. Unable to physically touch him, his attempts failed. Jack had a death grip around the old man's neck. He squeezed until his eyes widened and the man displayed a devilish grin before he slumped over in his rocking chair.

A look of panic rose on Jack's face. He knew he couldn't stay there after what he had just done. Jack quickly ran to his car and sped off. Jackson saw flashes of what had to have been Jack's nightmares. The same stages of sleepless nights and drinking to numb the pain.

Jackson could have ended up killing Carmen had she not left. It all made sense now, this was a life-long dysfunctional gene in this family. His father killed his own father. Which tormented Jack into becoming evil himself. Jackson blinked and all was back normal. He had taken a trip into the past.

Remembering the house in the vision, Jackson quickly found some paper and a pen to jot it down. After a night's rest, he planned on finding the house. He had so many unanswered questions. Such as why did Jack fear his father in the first place.

The next day, Jackson wasted no time finding the address. Just like in the vision the rocking chair was still on the porch.

"Jackson, what are you doing here?"

"You see him too, must have been daddy. I see him sometimes too every time I stop by and check on this house. He don't harm nothing, he just makes his presence known."

Walter smiled.

"Thanks for the number, you be careful uncle Walter in that house."

Jackson told him as the old man reappeared on the porch in the rocking chair. Aunt Stella lived out of state so he decided to call her up right away. After hearing the entire story Jackson was speechless.

It was no wonder Jack was the black sheep of his family. The things he heard was enough to make even Jackson's life seem like a fairytale. Jackson wouldn't know how to cope if he endured what his father had. Aunt Stella even felt bad for repeating some of the things he went through. Jack told her everything up to his last days on earth.

1950 Rural Mississippi

"You ain't got a damn thing to say to me!"

Jack heard his father yell.

It was dark out and his father had been out drinking again. He had never heard them fight like that before. The bedroom door flew open and Jack was snatched up from under the covers. Belt in hand, his father struck him over and over.

"This motherfucker eating in my home and carries another man's blood. I want him out and I mean now!"

His voice boomed.

Young Jack didn't know what was going on. His father aimed a double barrel shot gun to his head.

"Unless you want me to blow your gotdamn head off you better keep walking till I say stop!"

He spat.

Leading him out into the back yard. Young Jack walked as tears ran down his face. He walked until he came to a shallow creek.

"Go on get in the water or I'll throw you into it."

He warned.

"Paw I.I..I can't swim."

Walter asked coming out of the house.

"Needed some answers uncle Walter. You know everything daddy did to me and my sisters really messed me up. What kind of childhood did my daddy have? He never spoke much about our grandparents."

Jackson told him.

"Daddy was pretty hard on Jack. Never whooped any of the rest of us but Jack, he beat him so much. It just didn't make any sense. Momma wouldn't say why nor did we question daddy for doing it. But Stella can tell you more than I can. They never tell me anything."

Walter laughed.

"You got aunt Stella's number?"

Jackson asked.

"Yeah come in for a sec while I go and get it for you."

Walter held the screen door open for him. Jackson stepped into the house and a tall man with red eyes rocked in a chair in the kitchen.

"Have some of them sausage links and grits over on the stove?"

Walter asked.

"No thanks," Jackson replied keeping his eyes on the old man.

Getting a better look, it was the same old man Jack strangled. The rocking chair stopped and the man stood. In a blink of an eye he was gone that fast. He just up and vanished out of thin air. Looking around the living room the old man was now walking up the hallway. Jackson stopped dead in his tracks and tried to show no fear.

The man started running towards him causing Jackson to run out of the house.

"What the fuck?!"

Jackson spat as his heart raced and chest heaved up and down.

"You okay?" Walter asked, handing him the paper with the number on it.

"There was an old man in that kitchen. Then he ran towards me from the hallway."

Jackson said.

Jack cried out pleading with him not to make him go in the creek. With a hard kick in his back, Jack went face first into the creek. Trying to come up for air he kicked and screamed.

"Please stop it! Don't let my baby drown! Lord Jesus help him!"

Jack's mother screamed.

The rest of the kids followed the screams. All began to weep watching Jack struggle to stay above water.

"Help my baby Lord don't let him drown please!"

Lucille wept.

"You want that bastard to live so bad, huh. Then take yo ass out there and save him!"

He yelled pushing Lucille, his wife into the water. She tried reaching out to Jack, but she couldn't swim herself.

"Momma heeeeeelp!"

Jack screamed as the water repeatedly swallowed him.

"Momma noooooo!"

Walter screamed in horror as she went under water. The neighbors next door came running gun in hand.

"What's going on back here?"

Mr. Bobby Ray asked.

"Daddy look he drowning!"

Bobby Ray Jr. Yelled and pointed out at the creek.

Dropping his gun Bobby Ray Sr. ran into the water and immediately pulled Jack out. Coughing up water Jack pointed at the creek. No words came out but Bobby Ray looked and saw a drowning woman.

Leaving Jack, he went back in to pull her out of the water. Lucille wasn't breathing at all and Bobby Ray went to perform CPR, until he was gazing down the barrel of a shotgun.

"Gone head and get way from round here before I blow yo head off nigga!"

"Get that gun out my daddy face!"

Bobby Ray Jr. spat aiming the .38 special at Jack's father. He and Jack were best friends and around the same age.

"Boy, you best use that gun or I swear for God you're going to sho'nuff wish ya had of."

He replied.

"Leave my boy be, your wife not breathing. All's I trying to do is help her that's it. Let me help and then I will be on my way."

Bobby Ray Sr said.

"She don't deserve to live and neither does her bastard child. She done laid down with my own blood. You hear me, my own blood! Lie to me to my face, let her die she earn the right to!"

He said with tears in his eyes.

"I can't do that, and deep down you don't want that for her."

Bobby Ray replied.

Placing both palms on Lucille's chest he pressed down and counted to three.

"Come on now! Come on back to us Lu!"

He said while alternating from chest compressions and blowing air into her mouth.

He did this for two minutes straight, before Lucille spit up water and gasped. She was in a daze, Jack's father returned into the house.

Lucille may have survived, but she had no idea what was in store for her. He made their lives a living hell. Jack had to pay for his mother's affair. The things he endured was enough to turn anyone's stomach.

A few days after the drowning incident. Jack came home from the schoolhouse. No one was home except for the old man. That had to be the first-time Jack was beat.

"Don't slam no doors in here! This my house ya here?"

He said causing Jack to tremble. Jack remained silent and went into his room to play. Not long after Jack was being beat by a metal wire hanger.

Jack was dragged into the kitchen by his legs. Placing a glove on, his father grabbed a piece of hot burning wood. Pressing it against Jack's back the boy howled in agony. Lucille heard the screams halfway up the street. Running home, she rushed into the house.

"I'm gone break you boy you will do as I say. Now go out and rake that yard."

He said as Jack quickly ran out of the kitchen.

Lucille was knocked down and beaten next. He violated her in such sickening ways. Forcing wire hangers up her vaginal region. As well as a broom handle and cake mixer utensils. Lucille could not bore anymore children after all she had endured.

She even attempted suicide a few times. Only he allowed her to do so much when it came to harming herself. He would tell her things like death is too easy for you.

Jackson felt bad for his father. Aunt Stella knew the truth, and that's why she was so defensive over her baby brother. Ending the call, after learning all of this, he needed a drink. This was going to be harder than he thought.

Chapter Two

Elijah

"I Know"

"Can I come inside please?"
Elijah asked.
The look on his girlfriend's face expressed exactly how she felt. Riley had thought the world of him. They had dreams of being married after he get his NBA contract. She would cheer him all the way to the top.

With dreams of having her own dental practice. They had their life all mapped out. College in a few years, move to L.A. and work on the goals they both wrote out. Only now things were different.

She wouldn't have Elijah's first child, there wasn't a fairytale wedding. Hell, they didn't even graduate high school yet. Now all of a sudden everything went left. Finding out his family really wasn't his family.

Then there's the whole fact that he cheated. To top it all off he had unprotected sex and the girl is pregnant. Who, by the way is living with him and his real mother.

Riley took all that in and it overwhelmed her. How could they move on from this? It was all way too much she would look crazy being with him. His entire life now consists of drama. Drama she wanted no parts of.

"Riley, please?"
He said grabbing her hand.
Snatching away, Riley took a deep breath before giving him a reaction about all he just said. Her stress levels were through the roof. All she could picture is a child that looked just like him. Tears began to fall from her eyes. Had she not been a good girlfriend.

They didn't have sex a lot but, whenever they did was he not satisfied? Riley second guessed herself about everything. Then she realized she wasn't to blame. Sure, they weren't a perfect couple but who is. They argued and would always fix things.

Riley didn't believe in not talking things out. Her parents were divorced and she hated how easily they each gave up.

Whenever girls were all in Elijah's face she remained standing. Not giving them the satisfaction of a reaction. She was secure in her relationship and knew her place. She never in a million years would think this would happen. He showed no signs of cheating and that is what confuses her the most. How could she not have known?

"Elijah, I told you before what I expected. If it was just the simple fact of you being with another girl, maybe I could get over it but this. Elijah, you could possibly have a child I can't accept that. I mean this really hurts. It was supposed to be me having your kids. Are you even excited about having a baby?"

She asked.

"No because it's not mine. Riley, look baby I messed up I know. You gotta believe me when I say that's not my baby."

Elijah said to her.

"How do you know for sure, you did have unprotected sex with her. See that means that there is a chance it is yours. Let's talk about the fact that you even fucked another girl. How would you feel if I slept with another guy Elijah? What if I got pregnant and said it might be yours or this other guy? You would have left me without thinking twice and you know it!"

Riley spat.

"Yeah, I would be upset but at the same time, I love you. Me being me I would stay and work it out."

He said.

"That is bullshit and you know it! Elijah, you cheated and she's pregnant. So how long you two been messing around and don't lie?""

Riley asked folding her arms across her chest.

"Are we really doing this?"

Elijah said running his hand over his face.

"Be a man and own up to your shit. Don't bitch up now, I mean you told me this much. Might as well tell it all so let's keep it a hundred. How long you been sleeping with her?"

Riley asked.

"Since July, alright!"

He said.

"How long you been talking to her?"

Riley asked.

"I talked to her like in May."

He said.

"Ohhh, so ya'll been chilling for a nice little minute. Why the fuck you didn't just break up with me if you were with her!?"

Riley yelled slapping him.

"I didn't want her like that I wanted you."

He said trying to hug her.

"No you didn't, you been with this girl four months probably longer. Then you gone say you wanted me. No, you thought you could fuck around with her. Then come back to me, nah it doesn't work like that. I told you how my exes did me. I told you about how I got cheated on. What you say I ain't like them dudes. Well I can't tell Elijah! Yeah niggas done hurt me but not like this. You got a whole baby on the way and think shit is sweet. I told you from jump I'm not playing stepmother for nobody. You might as well go be with her. Like on some real shit I'm done. We a wrap and I'm dead ass!"

She spat.

"I mean so what you saying?"

Elijah asked almost in tears.

"I'm saying Riley ain't a dumb bitch anymore! I am not about to be no stepmother. She can have you, ya'll go be cute shit, go play house. You got me all the way messed up. Matter of fact get away from my house!"

She yelled.

Elijah tried pulling her into his arms. You would think someone so short wouldn't put up a fight. Especially, since Elijah was six- three to her measly five-two. Riley's brother Devin heard the commotion.

"What's going on?"

He asked looking at his sister then to Elijah.

"You wanna tell your buddy the reason we not together, or should I?"

Riley laughed sarcastically.

"It was a mistake and I told you the girl is lying."

Elijah said.

"She lying about being pregnant by you. Even though you two been fucking around four or five months already. Oh okay, yeah right nigga please!"

Riley spat.

"E, really my nigga?!"

Devin said shaking his head.

"It ain't like that D. The girl lying, don't get me wrong I messed up but that's not my baby. I'm getting a DNA test and I will prove it."

Elijah said stepping off the porch.

"Yeah well I'm single and that's your problem I'm over it all."

Riley said walking into her house.

"D, please talk to her you gotta believe me. We go way back, you know I wouldn't play about nothing like this."

Elijah said.

"This is exactly why I didn't want you with my sister. If you were gone be doing you fam. Yo ass could have left her alone then."

Devin spat before going into the house and shutting the door.

Elijah begin walking home. His whole entire world was crashing. Riley was his heart and he couldn't see himself without her. He had always known that Riley would be his wife. For years, he tried to be with her. Riley just didn't like any of her brother's friends.

It wasn't until last year he had finally worn her down. They clicked instantly and now it was all over. Juniqua was only supposed to be a one-time thing. After he got to know her he started to fall for her.

Like Riley, she too had been hurt. Elijah didn't want to hurt neither of them. Now that he has, the question is who will he fight for? He lied about everything to Juniqua. With Riley, he lied throughout the relationship by being unfaithful.

Thinking about a DNA test. Elijah wasn't sure if he wanted to even know whether it was his child. How was he going to play ball with a baby? How could Riley consider giving him a second chance. If in fact the baby was his.

"This shit is all fucked up!"

He spat while texting Riley how sorry he was.

Back at his house Juniqua was in the living room. Watching TV, she didn't say a word as Elijah sat down on the couch. Now that she would be attending the same school as him, he figured he tell her about Riley.

"Listen my girl knows about everything. We need a DNA test as soon as we can make it happen. I'm not trying to lose my girl over this bullshit."

He told her.

"You act as if this is my fault! I wouldn't have dated you had I known you even had a girlfriend. Does your girl know about you giving me a fake name? This was all your fault Elijah not mine!"

Juniqua said.

"Yeah ok Juicy, and I'm sorry damn why is all this shit even necessary?"

He asked wishing this would all go away.

"Had I not come to your friend's house, were you ever going to tell me the truth?"

She asked.

"Eventually, I wasn't expecting to fall for you. My feelings were real until I found out all that about you and these other dudes."

Elijah said.

"Elijah not once did I cheat on you. I told you before I wouldn't do that to you."

Juniqua said.

"That still don't change the fact that you been with too many guys. Why you didn't tell me about all that? You have any idea how stupid you had me looking?"

Elijah said.

"I tried to several times and that was the past Elijah. all of it was before I met you."

She said.

"Look you knew I had a right to know."

Elijah spat.

"You right and I'm sorry for not giving you details on everything I did before meeting you."

"Momma you didn't even knock though."

He said putting on his pants.

"This my damn house, I don't have to knock on no door! Last I checked your room was upstairs. What the hell were you doing in here?"

Joy asked.

"I'm so sorry Miss Joy it just sort of happened."

Juniqua said.

"I see now, that you two can't live under the same roof. You know what Elijah until this baby comes. Yo disrespectful ass will be at your uncle Jackson's house. Running my damn blood pressure up. Change these damn sheets and wash your asses!"

Joy yelled before leaving out of the room.

"Momma why I gotta leave?"

Elijah asked.

"Yo best bet is to not say shit to me boy. You really gone ask me that?"

She fussed.

Elijah knew she was beyond mad, his mother was hot. Not that he wasn't either he didn't even finish. Taking the covers off the bed both Elijah and Juniqua couldn't stop looking at each other. They started laughing at the whole situation.

"This is crazy I can't believe this man."

Elijah said laughing.

"I can't believe your mom walked in on us."

Juniqua blushed.

"That's because yo ass was all loud. Gave you that good "D" you couldn't help it."

Elijah smiled.

"Oh please, if anything I was putting it on you. Could have sworn you were saying ooh Juicy it's so good."

Juniqua mocked his moans.

"Wait till later on we gone see."

He said.

"Is that a threat?"

She asked flirting back.

"All facts baby you gone see."

He said giving her a wink.

Juniqua said with sarcasm.

"Had I known how you get down it wouldn't have got this far."

He spat.

"Go ahead, because I have been called trifling, bitch, that, slut, buss-down you name it. Say exactly whatever it is you wanna say. I can take it but what I can't take is you denying our child! Before I met you, I was in a dark place and you knew that. I'm glad we met, you showed me more than just jumping in bed with me. You cared enough to listen to me. Even if it was a lie, I never felt love before you. That's why it hurt like hell when you went ghost on me. I was back being all alone again. I won't force you to be a father. As soon as Miss Joy gets home I'm leaving. I don't want to be anywhere near someone that doesn't want my child."

She said before heading in the guest room.

Elijah was torn between being with Riley or being a father. He knew Juniqua wasn't lying. It would be wrong to let her raise a child alone. Then there was the fact that she had bodies on her. He saw the video of her with other guys. How could he cuff a loose girl?

Past or not he would be the laughing stock of his school. Knocking on the guest room door. Elijah decided to man up and do the right thing.

"Aye listen, we just gone take a test. If it's mine, I got you I'll take care of mine."

He said.

Juniqua opened the door, she hugged him happy to hear that.

"That's fine."

She said.

"Now I gotta figure out how to get my girl back. Riley not even returning my calls."

He said.

"Maybe after a while y'all could work things out over time."

Juniqua said.

"I hope so we were supposed to be going to the 21 Savage concert next week." He sighed.

"Can I ask you something?"

She said.

"What up?"

Elijah sensed she was hesitant.

"Did you ever love me or was it all just game?"

She asked.

"I did before I saw that tape, I was even thinking about leaving Riley."

Elijah said being honest.

"Had it not been for my past we would still be together?"

She asked.

"Maybe," he shrugged.

"Oh," she replied looking down at her feet.

"I do miss us talking."

He told her.

"Me too, you really hurt me by being an ass."

She said pushing him in his chest.

"I'm sorry for real."

Elijah said kissing her forehead.

"We should stop before we do something you're going to regret."

Juniqua said stepping back.

"It's like that now?"

He said taking a step towards her.

"You have a girl and I don't want to come between that."

She said above a whisper.

"Guess you right then I'ma go see what Antwon doing. You good, you need anything before I go?"

He asked her.

"I'm cool."

She replied.

"Alright hit my line if you need anything."

Elijah said before turning to leave.

As bad as she wanted him she fought the urge to jump his bones. Elijah had to adjust himself, he was horny and Riley wasn't a fan of him. Knowing sex would only complicate things with someone new. He figured why not hook up with Juniqua one last time. Heading back to the guestroom. Elijah shut the door behind him, causing Juniqua to jump.

"What's wrong?"

She asked as he stepped to her.

"I miss you."

He said kissing her lips.

Running his hands down her body he pulled her close to him. Juniqua couldn't deny that she didn't miss his touch either. It drove her crazy to see him and not be able to touch him.

"What about your girl?"

She asked as he laid her down on the bed.

"We not together right now so don't trip."

He told her while sliding down her jeans.

Spreading her thighs Elijah wasted no time easing between them. They held each other as their bodies reintroduced themselves.

"I missed you so much."

Juniqua moaned.

"I missed you too."

Elijah said.

The bed springs began to squeak. Elijah nor Juniqua paid any attention to hearing the front door slam. They were too far gone and caught up in the moment.

Joy and Jasmine were back from the store. Joy rushed to go pee after holding it in for so long. Passing the guest bedroom she heard moans.

"I know damn well they ain't fucking in my house!"

Joy said snatching the bedroom door open.

Joy couldn't believe her eyes. There's her sixteen-year-old son naked as the day she birthed him. In doggy style position with Juniqua bent over.

"I know good and gotdamn well you two not fucking under my roof! If you don't get your trifling asses dressed. Elijah, you know better and Lil girl you on very thin ice."

Joy spat.

"Momma I can explain it ain't even like that."

Elijah said.

"How is it Elijah? Please tell me all about how you accidentally got caught sleeping with your already pregnant ex. Or whatever the hell it is you two are to one another!"

Joy said.

Juniqua said with sarcasm.

"Had I known how you get down it wouldn't have got this far."

He spat.

"Go ahead, because I have been called trifling, bitch, that, slut, buss-down you name it. Say exactly whatever it is you wanna say. I can take it but what I can't take is you denying our child! Before I met you, I was in a dark place and you knew that. I'm glad we met, you showed me more than just jumping in bed with me. You cared enough to listen to me. Even if it was a lie, I never felt love before you. That's why it hurt like hell when you went ghost on me. I was back being all alone again. I won't force you to be a father. As soon as Miss Joy gets home I'm leaving. I don't want to be anywhere near someone that doesn't want my child."

She said before heading in the guest room.

Elijah was torn between being with Riley or being a father. He knew Juniqua wasn't lying. It would be wrong to let her raise a child alone. Then there was the fact that she had bodies on her. He saw the video of her with other guys. How could he cuff a loose girl?

Past or not he would be the laughing stock of his school. Knocking on the guest room door. Elijah decided to man up and do the right thing.

"Aye listen, we just gone take a test. If it's mine, I got you I'll take care of mine."

He said.

Juniqua opened the door, she hugged him happy to hear that. "That's fine."

She said.

"Now I gotta figure out how to get my girl back. Riley not even returning my calls."

He said.

"Maybe after a while y'all could work things out over time." Juniqua said.

"I hope so we were supposed to be going to the 21 Savage concert next week." He sighed.

"Can I ask you something?"

She said.

"What up?"

Elijah sensed she was hesitant.

"Did you ever love me or was it all just game?"

She asked.

"I did before I saw that tape, I was even thinking about leaving Riley."

Elijah said being honest.

"Had it not been for my past we would still be together?"

She asked.

"Maybe," he shrugged.

"Oh," she replied looking down at her feet.

"I do miss us talking."

He told her.

"Me too, you really hurt me by being an ass."

She said pushing him in his chest.

"I'm sorry for real."

Elijah said kissing her forehead.

"We should stop before we do something you're going to regret."

Juniqua said stepping back.

"It's like that now?"

He said taking a step towards her.

"You have a girl and I don't want to come between that."

She said above a whisper.

"Guess you right then I'ma go see what Antwon doing. You good, you need anything before I go?"

He asked her.

"I'm cool."

She replied.

"Alright hit my line if you need anything."

Elijah said before turning to leave.

As bad as she wanted him she fought the urge to jump his bones. Elijah had to adjust himself, he was horny and Riley wasn't a fan of him. Knowing sex would only complicate things with someone new. He figured why not hook up with Juniqua one last time. Heading back to the guestroom. Elijah shut the door behind him, causing Juniqua to jump.

"What's wrong?"

She asked as he stepped to her.

"I miss you."

He said kissing her lips.

Running his hands down her body he pulled her close to him. Juniqua couldn't deny that she didn't miss his touch either. It drove her crazy to see him and not be able to touch him.

"What about your girl?"

She asked as he laid her down on the bed.

"We not together right now so don't trip."

He told her while sliding down her jeans.

Spreading her thighs Elijah wasted no time easing between them. They held each other as their bodies reintroduced themselves.

"I missed you so much."

Juniqua moaned.

"I missed you too."

Elijah said.

The bed springs began to squeak. Elijah nor Juniqua paid any attention to hearing the front door slam. They were too far gone and caught up in the moment.

Joy and Jasmine were back from the store. Joy rushed to go pee after holding it in for so long. Passing the guest bedroom she heard moans.

"I know damn well they ain't fucking in my house!"

Joy said snatching the bedroom door open.

Joy couldn't believe her eyes. There's her sixteen-year-old son naked as the day she birthed him. In doggy style position with Juniqua bent over.

"I know good and gotdamn well you two not fucking under my roof! If you don't get your trifling asses dressed. Elijah, you know better and Lil girl you on very thin ice."

Joy spat.

"Momma I can explain it ain't even like that."

Elijah said.

"How is it Elijah? Please tell me all about how you accidentally got caught sleeping with your already pregnant ex. Or whatever the hell it is you two are to one another!"

Joy said.

"Momma you didn't even knock though."

He said putting on his pants.

"This my damn house, I don't have to knock on no door! Last I checked your room was upstairs. What the hell were you doing in here?"

Joy asked.

"I'm so sorry Miss Joy it just sort of happened."

Juniqua said.

"I see now, that you two can't live under the same roof. You know what Elijah until this baby comes. Yo disrespectful ass will be at your uncle Jackson's house. Running my damn blood pressure up. Change these damn sheets and wash your asses!"

Joy yelled before leaving out of the room.

"Momma why I gotta leave?"

Elijah asked.

"Yo best bet is to not say shit to me boy. You really gone ask me that?"

She fussed.

Elijah knew she was beyond mad, his mother was hot. Not that he wasn't either he didn't even finish. Taking the covers off the bed both Elijah and Juniqua couldn't stop looking at each other. They started laughing at the whole situation.

"This is crazy I can't believe this man."

Elijah said laughing.

"I can't believe your mom walked in on us."

Juniqua blushed.

"That's because yo ass was all loud. Gave you that good "D" you couldn't help it."

Elijah smiled.

"Oh please, if anything I was putting it on you. Could have sworn you were saying ooh Juicy it's so good."

Juniqua mocked his moans.

"Wait till later on we gone see."

He said.

"Is that a threat?"

She asked flirting back.

"All facts baby you gone see."

He said giving her a wink.

Elijah put the covers in the washer. Juniqua showered while Joy lectured Elijah. She was in the kitchen pacing back and forth.

"You have no respect for me or yourself neither one of y'all! If you think I'm gone just help raise your kid, you are gladly mistaken. You will be in your child's life! If you can lay down and make it then yo ass can man up and take care of it. I ain't for all of this, I don't know what you thought this was. This house is not going to be for shacking up or for babies to be running around in. Both of y'all got so much energy, I wanna see some job applications filled out."

Joy said.

"Momma I'm gone look for a job and I promise it won't happen again.""

Elijah told her.

"So what the hell are you two doing, are you together now?"

"No, we just cool. Me and my girlfriend Riley are working things out."

He said.

"Elijah why the hell are you sleeping with her if you don't plan on being with her. How dumb do you sound boy! If you not gone be with her then don't play with her feelings."

Joy spat.

"Mom she already knows about Riley, I told her."

He said.

"Lord Jesus, so she just proud to be a damn fool. You stupid too for doing the dumb shit. You are confusing her and the other girl isn't going to be okay with you sleeping with your baby momma."

Joy said.

"At least he straight, hell nephew got two girls. I rather have that then to deal with what I'm dealing with."

Jasmine said.

"Really Jas, I do not condone him being a thot."

Joy said.

"Momma why I gotta be a thot? That's hurtful ma, you can't be calling yo only child a thot."

Elijah said dramatically.

"Shut up because that is exactly what you acting like, a male thot."

Joy laughed.

"Mom it ain't even like that."

Elijah said.

"Look if you won't tell her the truth I will."

Joy said looking at Elijah sternly.

"It's only right."

Jasmine said agreeing.

"Aunt Jas and mom, how can I do that without hurting one of them."

He said.

"The truth is better than a lie any day."

Jasmine told him.

"I Will eventually but not right now."

Elijah shrugged.

"The longer you keep up this lie, the worst it will get. Just tell her the truth and put an end to all this drama."

Joy told him.

Juniqua listened intently before walking into the kitchen where they were talking. She wanted to hear exactly what Elijah's truth was and what he had to say.

"I was going to at least wait to see if the baby is mine."

He replied.

"Son you're using her and that's not right. I understand you didn't intend for it to go as far as it has. Right now, you don't know what you want. If Riley is truly the one you say you want to be with then nothing should stop you from making things right. Unless, you do have feelings for Juniqua. I told you already, ya should have kept your peter to yourself if that was the case. Riley would be stupid for staying after all of this. Then for you to keep dragging her along with it. This is only going to end bad and I do mean real bad."

Joy fussed.

"I will tell her we can't mess around anymore. Riley is who I want to be with. If the baby is mine I will help but that's it."

He said.

Juniqua was hurt once again by his words. Here she was thinking they could be a happy family. Once again, she felt as if her heart had been ripped out. Living here would only make matters worse. Walking into the kitchen, Elijah was the first to speak.

"Hey, can we talk for a sec?"

He said.

Juniqua nodded and followed him outside. They started walking up the street. Juniqua's heart raced, she already knew what was coming.

"You know I didn't mean for all this to happen but..."

He stopped walking and said.

"I know, I mean I should have known you wouldn't want to be with someone like me."

Juniqua replied.

"It's nothing wrong with you Juicy. I just been with Riley longer and we just got that bond. Or we had shot, it was getting bad and that's when I met you. I just wish I had met you first. Feels like my loyalty belongs with her but, then part of me wants to be with you."

He said.

"Elijah if it's that hard to choose between us just choose her. I'm sick of being your second choice. You basically just said I was your girl after you and her start having problems."

Juniqua cried.

"I told you already what I felt about you was real. You the one that kept secrets from me. Had you been real about your body count."

He shrugged.

"Being real! Elijah, you lied about everything, your name, your relationship, even where you live! Don't even go there about being real. I tried telling you and what you say, Juicy it doesn't matter I'm your man now."

She mocked his voice.

"That was before I knew half of Mississippi had you!"

He yelled causing people to stare.

"Fuck you Elijah!"

She spat walking off.

"We already done that remember?"

He said before turning around to walk back to the house.

Sitting on the porch, Elijah knew he had said too much and hurt Juniqua. His mother was right he didn't know who he wanted. Had he told Juniqua the truth they could be together. Pride is what made him choose Riley.

Elijah rather be unhappy with Riley than to be made fun of by being with Juniqua. In his eyes being with her would make him look like a fool.

Rather than go back to Elijah house. Juniqua decided to go over her cousin's house. She could live there and get a job and save up before the baby comes. All without being around Elijah.

The last person Juniqua expected to see was Antwon. Who she couldn't stand, and ever since she refused to sleep with him, Antwon had turned into a complete asshole.

"Damn juicy let me holla at you!"

He yelled.

Rolling her eyes, she pretended she didn't hear him. She tried telling Elijah about Antwon trying to get with her but he never took it serious. Walking up, Antwon wrapped his arms around her waist. Thrusting his pelvis up against her ass. Juniqua pushed him away and was ready to slap him.

"Stay the Fuck off of me!"

She spat.

"Damn juicy what's up with you?"

He smiled.

"What do you want Antwon?"

She asked annoyed.

"You know exactly what I want, give a nigga a chance. Straight up you should have been my girl. That nigga Elijah stupid for letting you go for real. See me, I would have cuffed you up."

He said.

"Type of friend is you, Elijah might not be perfect but at least he not fake!"

Juniqua spat.

"Please his ole bitch ass couldn't even be real enough to tell you his real name. On top of that he knows that's his baby. Does he claim it though? Hell naw, cause the nigga a straight up mark. If I ever have a child, you know I will never deny my seed. That's some ole bitch ass shit."

He said.

"Well once we get a test he will see that I wasn't lying. All I care about is raising my child. I could give two fucks about Elijah or another nigga."

Juniqua said.

"Man I'm telling you, he still not gone take care of it. Hell, he didn't even bring you out in public. Ya'll whole relationship was on hush. Even when ya'll was in your hometown he still didn't go out in public with you."

Antwon said.

"It doesn't matter we not together nor do I want him. I sure as hell don't want you either."

Juniqua said as she kept walking headed to her cousin house.

"Fuck you too then bitch!"

Antwon spat.

She knew that was coming before he even said anything. Why on earth would she get involved with her ex-boyfriend's best friend? She had never been that type of girl. Not now not ever and her word was bond.

As bad as she wanted to tell Elijah. She knew he wouldn't believe her. Just like last time Antwon dirty ass would turn things around. Making him look like he wouldn't do anything like that.

Knocking on her cousin's door she waited for an answer. When her cousin did finally open the door, they hugged. She planned to tell her cousin the whole story. Who knows maybe her aunt would feel sorry for her and let her stay.

Elijah tried calling Riley over and over, getting nothing but the voicemail. This was going to be a lot harder than he thought.

Chapter Three

Joy

"Taste My Ice Cream"

"Have you heard from Jackson?"

Joy asked Jasmine as soon as Elijah and Juniqua left out.

"No not in a few days, since he started working at Murphy's. That warehouse has him working long nights."

Jasmine replied.

Joy's phone rung and it was Nathan calling again. She had purposely been avoiding him since the funeral. It didn't feel right talking to him since she was talking to Charlene.

"Somebody blowing you up, your phone been ringing off the hook. Go ahead and give me all the tea."

Jasmine said.

"It's Nathan we accidentally kissed. Remember when we all saw him in the store? Then you and Carmen flaked on me afterwards. When I met up with him later that night, he told me he was in love with me back before I left for college."

Joy said mumbling on the last part.

"He said what Joy?"

Jasmine had to sit her cup down.

"Jas, we were friends and I don't see him like that."

Joy shrugged.

"Joy, why are you so bent on not going out with him or any guy for that matter."

Jas said.

"For one I like women, and Charlene and I are sort of talking."

Joy said.

"Listen sis, if daddy hadn't have done what he did. Do you think you would be into girls? You practically still a virgin. What happened to you wasn't fair Joy. Who knows what life you could have had. I love my nephew dearly he is the only good thing from it all. Honestly sis, I think you should just give men a try first. You said yourself every relationship you had failed. Maybe it's a sign, just go out it doesn't have to be Nathan either.

No matter if you do end up with a woman. He has been there from the beginning he's your friend."

Jasmine said.

Joy thought about what her sister said. She made a lot of sense he was her best friend. If anyone could set her up with a guy it was Nathan. He knew what she liked and what irritated her. All the talks they had as kids he knew enough.

"I do miss having him as a friend. You are right, we go way back and I shouldn't shut him out."

Joy said picking up her phone.

Nathan was surprised she even called back.

"Joy?"

He asked just to be sure it was in fact her calling back.

"Hey sorry I been missing in action, what's up?"

Joy said sounding upbeat.

Nathan was lost for words, she actually was talking to him.

"Um…no, it's no big deal. How have you been? I was just checking up on you."

He said.

"Being back home feels weird and the whole thing with Elijah back in my life. It's all a big adjustment. Speaking of my son, walked in on him having sex. Could you give me pointers on how to handle that as a parent?"

Joy asked.

Choking on his soda Nathan was as shocked to hear that as well.

"Damn J, I don't know what I would do. I'm not at that point with my kids yet. Thank God they are not sexually active and young."

He laughed.

Joy couldn't help but laugh even though earlier she was so mad she could ring her son's neck.

"Speak of the devil he's walking in the house now. You should really talk to him before I lose my mind."

Joy said.

"Ma, me and Juniqua got into it and Antwon said she over her cousin house. I think she staying over there now."

Elijah said.

"What did you do now boy, probably hurt her feelings. Just get out my sight because I could slap the hell out of you. Now you know she's pregnant you gone stress her out."

Joy fussed.

"You need me to come over and have a word with him? I was just about to head to the gym anyway."

Nathan said.

"Yeah thanks I'll text you the address."

Joy replied.

"I can be on my way soon as you give me the address."

He said.

"Ok see you when you get here."

Joy said hanging up and texting him the address.

"Go get cleaned up for dinner Elijah! Don't think for a second you not grounded either."

Joy yelled.

"Let me go see what David has to say, he wants to meet up. I will call you if I need you sis."

Jasmine told her while putting on her coat.

"Alright sis, love you and be careful especially since you carrying my future niece or nephew."

Joy walked her out.

Nathan's truck pulled up just as Jasmine was leaving. Joy stood on the porch watching him get out of his truck. Her heart raced as his tall frame came towards her. His muscles flexed with every step. Brown skin the color of cinnamon looking smoother than ever.

That right dimple that displayed in his cheek caused her to smile. Those dark brown eyes never looked sexier than they did right now. His cologne tickled her nose. Licking his full perfect lips, he said, "Hello."

Joy never felt like a young girl crushing until now.

"Hey you, I see you are gym ready."

Joy replied looking at his long gym shorts and skin tight training tank. Long Jordan socks and a fresh pair of Jordan sneakers.

Embracing him, his strong arms wrapped around her effortlessly. Bodies pressed up against one another neither wanted to let go.

"Why are you so freakishly tall or have I shrunk or something?"

Joy teased.

"You have gotten small, city done caused you to shrink."

He laughed.

"You hungry? I'm making my mother's famous fried chicken."

Joy asked as they walked into the house.

"See you wrong, I was supposed to work out. You know fried chicken is my weakness."

He smiled.

"So is that a yes?"

She asked.

"How could I say no to that."

He replied sitting down on the sofa.

"I haven't finished unpacking everything so excuse the boxes."

Joy told him.

"It's all good, I can help if you need me to."

Nathan said picking up a photo album off the coffee table.

"Why do you still have this picture? I was butt ugly."

Nathan said laughing.

"What picture?"

Joy asked standing over him to see the pic.

It was a picture of them at a church banquet. They were no more than six or seven years old. Nathan was missing both of his front teeth smiling brightly in the picture. Joy was hugging him and smiling just as bright as he was.

"I love this picture of us. I was cute, momma straighten my hair that Sunday. You got mad at me this day because I let Fred Fletcher push me on the swing."

Joy laughed.

"That's because that was my job. He was obsessed with you so I did you a favor by scaring him away."

Nathan said.

"Oh really, yet buck tooth Sharon was all up in your face. Did I scare her off, in fact I didn't say anything to your little fan club."

Joy rolled her eyes hitting Nathan in the back of his head.

"Hey, watch that! You can't be abusing me now."

He said pulling her into his lap tickling her. Elijah walked in the living room watching them two carry on like a love-struck couple.

"What's up coach?"

He said getting their attention.

"Oh hey Elijah, I was just about to ask where you were."

Nathan said as Joy jumped up off of his lap.

"I'm going to let you two talk and get this chicken started."

Joy said fleeing to the kitchen.

Elijah saw how embarrassed his mother was, her face was red.

"What's up with you and my mom?"

Elijah asked defensively.

Judging by the bass in his voice Nathan sensed that Elijah was upset.

"Oh we go way back, see this picture right here. Me and your mother have been best friends for years."

Nathan showed him the picture.

"That's all cool but she's off limits, that's my mother."

Elijah said.

Nathan saw that his fists was balled up and knew he was taking things out of context.

"Listen son, me and your mother are just friends we go way back like I was saying."

Nathan said.

"I ain't ya son!"

Elijah spat.

"Elijah that's enough! We are friends that's it, do not be disrespectful."

Joy said.

"I'm not, I just know his angle. He hooks up with all the players' mothers. Ain't that right coach, but not mine. I'll be damn if I let you play my mother."

Elijah spat.

"Boy watch your language we are still your elders."

Joy said.

"Listen, I can assure you it's not like that with your mother and I."

Nathan said.

"Good keep it that way."

Elijah said before walking out of the room.

"Boy you have some nerve, dictating like you pay bills!"

Joy fussed.

"Did I miss something? I never seen him so defensive like that."

Nathan said.

"Now you see what I mean. What am I going to do with this boy?"

Joy said sitting on the arm of the sofa.

"Just let him blow his steam, I will talk to him once he calms down."

Nathan said.

"Exactly how many mothers have you slept with?"

Joy asked.

"Can we not talk about this right now."

Nathan said wanting to change the subject.

"Must have been a lot, I see hasn't much changed."

Joy said heading back into the kitchen.

Nathan ran his hand down his face, he knew Joy was upset. Walking into the kitchen he tried to explain.

"Listen, after my divorce I was lost. I bedded a few women more than I should have. I was in a dark place, but then I got my shit together. Joy you know me, if I were lying I wouldn't be able to look at you right now."

Nathan said looking into her eyes.

"How many?"

Joy asked folding her arms in front of her.

"Five maybe six but it meant nothing."

Nathan said.

"That's a lot Nathan. God, no wonder he was thinking you were trying to get with me."

Joy said.

"So what are you saying that the kiss meant nothing?"

Nathan said.

"Of course it did, but it's not like we will ever be anything more than friends. You said yourself that we go way back. Plus, I was hoping you could introduce me to one of your male friends. Give the straight life a shot."

Joy shrugged.

"Wow let me get this straight. I pour my heart out and you expect me to be your homie and hook you up with another nigga? Fuck that! You wanna date men now, find a nigga on ya own."

Nathan spat before walking out the kitchen.

"Are you for real mad or are you playing with me right now?"

Joy asked following him into the living room.

"Does it look like I'm playing?"

He said as his chest did a rise and fall. His jaw muscle flexed and the frown on his face said it all.

"Nathan we were best friends, do you really wanna risk not being friends for another thirteen years."

Joy said.

"You right, look I should go."

He said heading towards the front door.

"Well okay, call me when you get a chance."

Joy said.

"Alright I will as soon as I leave the gym."

He told her.

Watching him pull out of the driveway. Joy shut the door once he drove off. Elijah walked back into the living room.

"Ma coach is a player don't fall for him."

He said.

"I have known Nathan a whole lot longer. Back when girls would lose their mind over him. So I know all about his charm and game. Sweetie momma can handle herself we are just friends. I have known him since forever. His mother and my mother were like sisters. You don't have anything to worry about."

Joy assured him.

"Alright ma, but if he try anything I might have to two piece him."

Elijah said punching the air.

"Well son you might wanna work on that right jab first. It looks a little sloppy, let ya ma show you how it's done."

Joy took a boxing stance.

"Ma why you can't just be a normal mom."

He said.

"Because, I'm different yup I'm different pull up to the scene with my ceiling missing."

Joy rapped the 2 Chainz verse.

"Here we go with the rapping."

Elijah said laughing.

After cooking and cleaning up, Joy went through a few more boxes. Tired from all of today's events Joy laid across her bed. Waking up to her phone ringing, she picked up.

"Hello?"

She answered half asleep.

"Sorry for waking you but I couldn't sleep."

The caller said.

"Nathan? Is everything alright?"

Joy asked.

"Yeah I thought about what you said. We can be friends, I don't wanna go years with us not talking."

He said.

"So is it safe to say that you gone hook me up with one of your male friends."

Joy said.

"Only if you hook me up with one of your lesbian friends. I like girls who like girls, two for one is good."

He said.

"Keep on and get hung up on."

Joy said.

"Oh now it's not funny anymore huh?"

He asked.

"Whatever, tomorrow can you change my oil? I done put all them miles on it. Just by driving it here I need to get some tires before it gets cold."

Joy said.

"I can do that. Aye guess who called me today? Remember eight grade when Ricky Thomas moved here. He hit me up said he might be moving back this way in a few months."

Nathan said.

"Lord you two together is a hot ass mess. Ugh I couldn't stand him, always undressing me with his eyes."

Joy laughed.

"That boy just as crazy now as he was then. I ended up relapsing today too, thanks to you."

He said.

"Whose mother did you sleep with?""

Joy spat.

"Is that what you think of me?"

Nathan said.

Joy didn't know what to say so she remained silent.

"For your information, after the gym I went and got chunky chip ice cream. The kind I use to get you to make you feel better."

He said.

"I'm sorry I didn't know, let's start over. What did you relapse on best friend?"

Joy asked.

"It's cool, I don't even feel like talking."

He said.

"Nathan!"

Joy said looking at her screen and saw that the call was still live.

"Oh, so you just going to stop talking to me. Just a big ole baby ugh?"

Joy said remembering when he would go hours not talking to her when they were younger. The longest they would go is an entire day. Prior to the time when she went away to college.

"Nathan bring me some ice cream. I haven't had any of Mr. Sylvester's ice cream in years."

Joy whined.

"Humph."

Nathan mumbled being stubborn.

"Nathan please?"

Joy asked really craving her childhood favorite ice cream.

"Its two in the morning Joy."

Nathan said.

She had to be out of her mind if she thought he was going to get out of his warm bed, to go give her ungrateful ass some of his ice cream at two in the morning.

"Pretty please?"

Joy said begging.

"You must be out yo damn mind."

He said.

"Fine be stingy then."

Joy said pouting.

"I will."

He replied not really paying her any mind.

It was dead silence with neither of them speaking. Nathan knew Joy was losing her mind over there. She couldn't stand being ignored and he knew it.

"Nathan how much do you want for that ice cream?"

Joy asked breaking the silence.

"Fat ass."

He laughed at how serious she was.

"No, for real Nathan stop playing and bring me some."

She said.

"Give me ten minutes, dang."

Nathan said getting up out of bed.

"That's why I love you!"

Joy said doing a little victory dance.

"I love you too, now hang up so I can get dressed."

He said smiling.

"No, its two in the morning you staying on the phone with me the entire time negro. That ice cream needs to get here safely. You might as well put me on speakerphone."

Joy said.

"Wow, so glad to hear how much you care about me!"

Nathan said sarcastically.

"Let me put some clothes on since you on your way."

Joy said just to mess with him.

"What you mean?"

He asked her.

"Now you know I sleep nude, always have since college."

Joy lied.

A loud crash in Nathan's background made Joy laugh.

"You okay over there?"

She asked damn near in tears from laughing so hard.

"You fucking with me ain't you?"

He asked.

"Yes, now hurry up I'm hungry."

Joy said.

"I shouldn't share with you."

He told her.

Talking smack to each other until he was pulling up. Joy greeted him at the door and led him to her room. She gestured for him to be quiet. As if they were sneaking around like teenagers. Once she closed and locked the door, Nathan kicked off his shoes and sat on her bed.

"I didn't want Elijah hearing us. You wanna watch something, the remote is on the nightstand over there."

Joy said.

Handing him a spoon as she turned off the light. Nathan turned to Dave Chapelle which was recorded on her DVR.

"This my shit! What you knew about Dave?"

He teased.

"Please Dave is a legend in comedy."

Joy said digging into the ice cream.

"You know, I really did miss this. Us chilling like old times, glad you moved back."

Nathan smiled.

"Me too it feels nice."

Joy smiled back.

"You wanna hear something funny?"

Joy asked him.

"What's up?"

Nathan said scooping up some ice cream out of the container.

"So Jasmine told me I'm basically still a virgin. Doesn't matter that I have damn near a grown man for a son."

Joy joked.

"You kind of are still a virgin if you think about it."

He said.

"Okay then I want you to take it."

Joy said.

Nathan coughed and begin to feel uncomfortable.

"Why…why you say that?"

He asked nervously.

"We both know, back then I would have chosen it to be you or Fred Fletcher.'"

Joy said.

"Say what?!"

Nathan spat upset she even mentioned that clown.

"I'm joking relax but it would have been you."

Joy told him.

"Oh yeah."

Nathan said running his hands through her hair.

Joy palms begin to sweat, she was so nervous and her heart raced.

"Would it be wrong if I said I always wondered about us?"

Joy said.

Leaning closer, Nathan cuffed her chin and looked into her eyes.

"Not at all."

He said inches from their lips touching.

"Nathan?"

Joy called his name.

"Yeah?"

He said still gazing at her.

"Hurry up and kiss me before I change my mind."

Joy said.

Nathan tasted her lips and Joy enjoyed the feel of his touch. Just like the first kiss they shared this kiss too felt perfect. Easing Joy back on the bed Nathan kissed down her neck on to her breast.

Feeling his lips and tongue pleased her nipples. Joy's pussy throbbed anticipating his touch. Nathan stripped her out of her panties and night pants so fast. She didn't even feel them come off.

The way he was kissing her breast had her in a trance. Easing lower he spread her pretty legs and eased his tongue between her second set of lips.

"Ohhhhhh!"

Joy moaned gripping the sheets.

The way Nathan had her feeling had to be against the law. He did a slow roll of his tongue which caused waves of pleasure. Joy's legs quaked and her back arched automatically. Nathan had control of her body like a remote.

Each spot he touched caused a reaction somewhere else on her body. Gripping the back of his head as he flicked his tongue on her clit. Joy was near that climax peak and she could tell it was going to be big.

Grabbing a pillow and throwing it over her face. She screamed into it and her body jerked uncontrollably.

"Nathan!"

Joy panted.

"Yeah baby?"

He answered enjoying the taste of her love raining down on his tongue.

"What are you doing to me?"

Joy said feeling another pleasure wave approaching.

"Giving you what I always wanted to give you."

He said before flicking his tongue faster and faster over her clit causing her eyes to roll to the back of her head. Placing the pillow back over her face Joy screamed to the heavens. The feeling of being overwhelmed was an understatement. What Joy was feeling was something much greater.

"Damn Nathan I didn't think it was going to feel this good shit!"

Joy said as the wave passed.

"You sure you want me to take it?"

He asked smiling that cocky smile.

"Oh you think you so good."

Joy blushed.

"I mean, the screams confirmed that baby."

He said confidently.

Joy being competitive, always loved a challenged. Sitting up, her legs was still shaking but she didn't care. She had to show him she wasn't nothing to play with either. Pulling him on top of her she pushed him and ended on topped of him. Picking up the melted ice cream and a spoon, Joy scooped up the melted ice cream. Pouring it on his chest down to his waist in a line.

Joy licked the ice cream off his body. Nathan moaned enjoying the feel of her tongue. Pulling down his shorts and boxers, his big dick sprang straight up. I

t was already hard as brick and Joy admired how good it looked. Grabbing the ice cream again she placed a spoonful in her mouth before sitting it on the dresser. Turning on some music Joy positioned herself between his legs.

Easing the head of his erection inside of her mouth. Nathan moaned as she went to work pleasing him. Feeling his toes curl Nathan was moaning so loud. Joy had to stop and reposition herself. Getting in the sixty-nine position Joy decided to put her pussy in his mouth to shut him up.

Going back to work they both went all out pleasing one another. Massaging his balls, Joy stroked him with her other hand. Holding her breath, she decided to try to take all of him inside her mouth. Feeling him hit the back of her throat.

Nathan gripped the sheets and was unable to hold it back any longer. The bitterness of his cum caused Joy to frown. Before she couldn't complain because he licked her into submission. Both were spent over what had just taken place. After all of that, he still hadn't taken it.

"You do know technically I'm still untouched below. I appreciate the orgasms though."

Joy smiled.

"Ain't this some shit, even after all we just did you still complain. Give me five minutes, shit I wasn't expecting all that."

Nathan said out of breath.

"I'm tired, we can try another time."

Joy said nestling in his arms.

They cuddled up and fell asleep until her alarm went off at five-thirty. Joy eyes fluttered open. Sunlight came in through the blinds causing them both to squint.

"Shit I forgot all about Elijah."

Joy said.

"Call me when he leaves for school. I'll let myself out."

Nathan said getting up out of bed and getting dressed.

"Wait, let me make sure he isn't up."

Joy said slipping on her silk robe.

Nathan rubbed against her from behind as she peeped out of the bedroom door.

"You not ready for another round, it's too soon."

Joy winked back at him.

"You must not know what they call me."

He flirted.

"What exactly do they call you? Better yet who calling you?"

Joy spat giving him a fair look that said I wish you would.

"Nothing baby relax."

He said not wanting to be back on her bad side.

Joy eased out in the hall with Nathan on her heels. Elijah must have still been sleep because his room was dark. Nathan kissed her on his way out and Joy watched him pull off. Like a teenager, she smiled and pranced around silly like.

After a hot shower, she cooked up some breakfast.

"I'm glad your company is gone, you two nearly woke up Elijah. I had to sleep out here with the TV up until y'all were done."

Jasmine said walking into the kitchen scaring Joy.

"Damn Jas, you nearly gave me a heart attack."

Joy said grabbing her chest.

"Funny sounded like Nathan gave you one last night."

Jasmine teased.

"Will you be quiet it was nothing."

Joy said making sure Elijah wasn't in ear shot.

Jasmine gave her a nigga please face.

"Okay it was good, real good but we're just friends. We talked about him being the one to take my virginity. We kissed and things heated up but we didn't fuck."

Joy said.

"What the hell were you two doing then? Sounded like a porno set last night."

Jas said.

"Ugh you make me sick but like I said we didn't fuck. We did other stuff and it was good."

Joy shrugged.

"So, you testing each part out one by one, huh."

Jasmine said laughing.

"Maybe but, we are just friends so it's no big deal."

Joy said.

"Please he done tasted your cookie, he is not going to want to be friends."

Jasmine said.

"I already told you, we talked and he will be ok with it."

Joy said making plates.

"Keep thinking that but trust and believe he's not going to be cool with it."

Jas said grabbing a piece of bacon and eating it.

"Cool with what? Morning ma, morning TT Jas."

Elijah said sitting at the table.

"Uh we were talking about your uncle Jackson being cool with seeing Carmen."

Joy lied.

"Oh yeah unk been moping around a lot."

Elijah said eating his pancakes.

"I hear that's contagious with men around here."

Jasmine said eying Joy.

"Ma you think you could talk to coach about letting me play starting five in next week's game. Since you two go way back maybe he will listen to you. The scouts for Ole Miss is going to be there. I need the spot light on me so I can get that scholarship."

Elijah said.

"Well nephew, yo ma got that covered they go back like legs right sis?"

Jasmine said.

Joy spit her orange juice out at Jasmine's remark.

"Say what?"

Joy said ready to strangle her sister.

"Auntie you mean go back like flats. Like four flats on a Cadillac not legs. Legs don't go back."

Elijah said.

"Apparently, they..."

Jasmine said before Joy cut her off.

"I can talk to him if you want I'm sure he would be reasonable."

Joy spoke over Jasmine.

Last thing she needed was for Nathan to get the wrong Idea.

Joy would straighten everything out quick fast and in a hurry.

She kept telling herself he would be fine with being just friends.

Chapter Four

Nathan

"I Wanna Be Your Man"

"What you telling me, is after the other night you just want to be friends?"

Nathan yelled.

Here they were being the loud couple in CVS. Joy had pulled another disappearing act on him. He spotted her in CVS and decided to give her a piece of his mind.

"Nathan, we talked about this and after everything we were going to be friends."

Joy said in a hush tone.

"That's before you sucked the soul out of my dick. Now you want us to go back to being friends? You think I'm going to be okay with you being with another nigga?"

Nathan said in a low voice.

"Why does it have to be all or nothing with you?"

Joy asked getting frustrated.

"I told you, I'm in love with you before any of this even happened. But yeah you right it is all or nothing. I refuse to keep hiding my feelings because you are unsure of what you want!"

He said.

"I want to give dating around a try. At least I'm up for dating men now with the help from you."

Joy joked.

"Good luck with that Joy."

Nathan said before leaving the store.

He was done chasing behind her. After everything they had been through, he still wasn't good enough for her. Getting in his truck his phone vibrated and Joy's name displayed across the screen. Sending her to voicemail he started up his truck and headed to the gym.

He needed to work out his frustrations. Nathan was headed inside of the fitness center. When he ran into one of his basketball players mother.

"Hey coach, haven't seen you in a while. "

She smiled.

"Lisa, hey how you been?"

Nathan spoke.

"Surprise you even remember my name."

She teased.

"I do...I just been so busy and an old friend of mine is back in town. I'm sorry if I led you on in any way."

Nathan said.

"Must be some friend, huh."

Lisa replied.

"We go way back and yes she means a lot to me."

He told her.

"I see, well if things don't work out you have my number."

Lisa said before walking away.

Nathan headed inside to lift some weights.

The situation with Joy was beginning to become stressful. After a long workout, Nathan went home and cleaned himself up. He needed to check on his kids. Melanie, his ex-wife constantly made sure to remind him just who ruined their marriage.

"So suddenly you decide to drop by and finally see your kids. What, did you put chasing hoes on pause?"

She spat.

"Mel come on, let's not argue today. Can I please just check on my family."

Nathan said with a sigh.

"Oh, after all the bitches you done put before us. Now you wanna play family man!"

She yelled.

"I fucked up, is that what you want me to say? Mel, I messed up and I know I hurt you. We can at least be civil for the kid's sake. I'm trying real hard to show you that I'm committed to be a better father."

Nathan said.

"Nathan, you moved us here and our marriage is a wreck. This divorce has drained me emotionally. Was I not good enough? What was it because every single night, I remember I was laying in bed alone? It was me who wondered if our failed marriage was my fault. Could I have done something different to cause you not to cheat and it hurt. It really does hurt to see the man you're in love with break your heart. Do you even know what tomorrow is Nathan?"

Melanie said sipping from her glass of wine.

"Of course, tomorrow is our anniversary."

Nathan replied.

"No correction tomorrow would have been our anniversary. We been divorced, what eight months now. Even after all the shit you put me through. I still decided to stay here with the girls. So that you could be active in their lives. Through it all I still cared enough to consider your feelings. I have to hear from friends how you just with all different sorts of women. Meanwhile, I can't even have a conversation with another man. Simply because I'm still stuck on your lying, cheating, trifling ass!"

Mel said through clenched teeth.

Grabbing the bottle of wine off the counter, Melanie threw the bottle at Nathan. Ducking the bottle, it shattered up against the nearby wall behind him.

"You don't give a damn about nobody but yo motherfuckin' self!"

She screamed.

Nathan tried to calm her down but it only made things worse.

"Get out!"

She yelled over and over.

Nathan took a step towards her and Melanie's eyes showed so much hurt.

"Don't you dare! Just get the fuck out now Nathan!"

She cried.

With a look of defeat, Nathan turned to leave. Things were going from bad to worst. Just a year ago, his marriage was perfect. Not exactly perfect, but it was okay. It felt as if something were missing in his life. Not knowing exactly what it was, Nathan decided maybe what he was missing was excitement.

He and Melanie met in college the beginning of sophomore year. Once he got with her he stopped hanging out. They got serious and everything happened so fast. Before he knew it, he was drafted into the pros. Mel was pregnant and she didn't believe in abortions. Not that he asked her to do such a thing.

His career was taking off and he had an amazing rookie year. Then his agent encouraged him to tie the knot. Giving Mel the fairytale like dream wedding. On the outside, it all looked perfect. Truth was, Nathan wasn't happy at all.

He loved his kids, each were a blessing. He also loved Melanie but the timing was way off. The money and fame only made matters worse. Everyone had their hand out and felt they deserved a cut. Overwhelmed, Nathan tried to reach out to Joy.

When the injury came, things really began to fall apart. With the injury came depression. Once the money stopped rolling in they had to downsize. Nathan was crashing fast and nobody understood his grief. No one knew what it felt like to be living out your dream only to have it shattered.

That was not a part of the plan. Drinking played a major part along with the infidelities. Nathan could have told her the truth. Instead, he manned up and did what he thought was right. He wasn't ready for marriage or kids but he accepted it. Sure, he was wrong for the lying and cheating. Taking full responsibility on behalf of that. How come he got no credit for all the good things he had done.

Reaching for the doorknob, Nathan's heart broke hearing his ex-wife crying. With tears of his own falling, he wiped his eyes and hopped into his truck. Checking his phone, he missed two more calls from Joy. As bad as he didn't wanna call her back he did. He could use a friend right about now.

"Hello?"

She answered on the second ring.

"You call?"

Nathan said unsure of what else to say.

"Yeah, um I don't want us to go back to the way we were. your friendship means a lot to me. All I was saying is let's just keep it on the friendship level. Anything more would be a huge risk. I don't want to ruin it based off some unsure emotions."

Joy said.

"Maybe we shouldn't be friends or anything at all. I have a lot of shit going on in my life right now. I can't add being your emotional punching bag to that. So it was good seeing you but I rather us keep it at hello and goodbye."

Nathan said.

"Well alright, if that is the way you want it."

Joy replied sounding disappointed.

Nathan ended the call and knew he had hurt her feelings. He had to end it like that or his feelings would eventually get in the way.

Driving back to his apartment Nathan was all alone. Being alone deep in thought didn't help at all. All he could think about was how much he messed up. Not just his career, it was his marriage and his friends even his daughters.

"I can't do shit right!"

He yelled flipping over the coffee table.

Nathan went on a rampage searching for a bottle of comfort. It didn't matter what brand or whether it was dark or light. He needed that forbidden liquid to comfort him. To wrap its warm embrace around him until he felt it flowing within him.

After destroying his apartment. Nathan found an old bottle of Jack Daniels. It must have been one he had over looked, when he was getting rid of all the alcohol from his apartment. Opening the almost empty bottle. Nathan was six months in of his sobriety. However, here he was willing to throw it all away because of the women in his life.

Placing the bottle to his lips, before he could sip the poison his phone rang. Looking at his phone it was Joy again. Not really wanting to talk he tossed the phone on his couch. Taking a deep breath, Nathan closed his eyes and placed the bottle to his lips.

"Nathan, can you just talk to me please! Where are you I'm in my car now?"

He heard Joy's voice.

Opening his eyes, Nathan sat the bottle down. He thought he was losing his mind and he hadn't even taken a sip to drink yet. Following her voice, it was coming from his cellphone. Picking up, he told her his address and waited outside for her.

He didn't trust himself alone with the bottle inside. Seeing her car pull up five minutes later. Nathan never been happier to see her.

"Are you alright?"

She asked walking towards him.

Joy hugged him and like a child Nathan broke down in her arms.

"I'm right here, you can tell me anything, what's wrong?"

Joy asked.

"Everything, it's my life, my kids, my ex-wife, even you. Everything that I love I eventually ruin Joy."

Nathan said.

"No that's not true Nate you didn't ruin me."

Joy replied.

"Then what happened to us after high school?"

He asked.

"I was going through other stuff remember. It was much deeper than Charlene and you two kissing. I needed to get away and I didn't tell you because I didn't want anyone to know the truth. I can finally move on, now that every secret I kept in is out."

Joy said.

"The only secret I had was being in love with you. Look how telling you turned out," he said.

"What you mean, we ate ice cream didn't we?"

Joy teased.

"No for real Joy it was supposed to be us going pro together. We supposed to be the real life love & basketball, remember?"

He said.

"Yeah, I remember. Are you sure you want that with me still? Would you have wanted me back then, if I had told you about all of the stuff with Elijah?"

Joy asked.

"I'm still here and that wasn't your fault."

He said.

"Nathan think about my emotional baggage. I'm in a healing process which some nights I still have nightmares. How do I know you won't freak out and up and leave?"

Joy said.

"Is that what you think, that I won't stick around?"

He laughed.

"Joy you should know better than that."

He replied.

"How about we take this slow. I don't want to rush into anything. You have to promise if we don't work, we will remain friends."

Joy said.

"I promise, but that doesn't mean that you shouldn't try and make this work."

He told her.

"I'm not just gonna be your girlfriend because we've known each other for years. You have to earn my love just like if you were someone else."

Joy said.

"I can do that but, I'm not gone lie I have some issues too. I almost took a drink earlier and had a meltdown. So, I hope you don't give up on me."

He said.

"You should know me better by now that I don't back down easily. Now can we go inside, its cold out here."

Joy said.

Nathan led her to his apartment and she looked at how trashed the apartment was.

"Ok, we might have to talk about this."

Joy said as she started picking up.

Nathan helped clean up as well. Once the apartment was clean, Joy headed home.

"Get some rest and I will see you later."

she hugged him goodbye.

Nathan knew they were taking things slow but this was at a snail's pace. They might as well have been just friends.

The next day at work Nathan was going over plays for the next game. Elijah was being so difficult with following instructions. He wondered if Joy told him about them being more than friends.

"Elijah what I need is for you to pass the ball. If you take too many shots we could risk losing the game. Now Jalen is wide open give him the ball. We want you to defend and for him to shoot. Together you two could be a force. Westbrook and Durant or Shaq and Kobe even Lebron and Kyrie. Be partners out on the court trust each other. You should be reading each other's mind out there."

Nathan yelled.

"I don't need no partner. I got thirty points last game coach."

Elijah bragged.

"Elijah, you not going to get far with that ego of yours. This is a team not superstar Elijah and Cantons bulldogs. So, either you play as a team player or not at all."

Nathan said.

"I'm the reason we destined for state. I ball my ass off each and every game and you talking like I'm one of these losers. I could play anywhere in the state. Canton High lucky I chose them to play for!"

Elijah spat.

"Son do you hear yourself, with that attitude you gonna end up by yourself. No team is going to want a bad sportsmanship player. Trust and believe I didn't get to the NBA on my skills alone. I played good by myself but with my team I was unstoppable."

Nathan told him.

"Unlike you I'm not gone go pro and choke. I got this, I don't need no partner or you!"

Elijah spat.

"Oh okay cause you big bad Elijah Johnson. The MVP, the destined NBA phenomenon. The greatest gift since MJ to the Bulls. Tell you what, since you so wonderful so nice on the court. I will step back and let you do your thing. Just not on this court, leave my gym your off the team."

Nathan said.

"What?!"

You can't kick me off the team, without me you all are garbage!"

Elijah yelled.

"Anybody agrees with Mr. Johnson here?"

Nathan asked his players.

The gym was quiet and Elijah stormed into the locker room. Nathan continued to have practice despite Elijah's poor team effort. It didn't take long before news got back to Joy. After practice, she wasted no time coming up to the school. Nathan made it to his truck before she let him have it.

"Really Nathan! You kicked him off the team for what?"

Joy asked.

"Look, I didn't plan on kicking him off the team. Elijah needs to know that there is no one man show. He wasn't being a team player, Joy. If you could see the way the boy was talking. You could see why I did what I did."

Nathan said.

"That still doesn't give you the right to kick the best player off the team. No matter what he did, you had no right to ruin his future still by kicking him off the team. You know he was counting on those scouts to be there."

Joy said.

"He won't make it with the way he going at it, by being a ball hog. He gloats around like he is the best thing to happen to this team since..."

Nathan went on but was cut off.

"All-star Nathan Williams. The cocky point guard who everyone wanted right. If I remember correctly, my son acts no different than you did when we were in high school. Yet you weren't kicked off the team, now were you?"

Joy spat.

"The boy needs discipline, something I possessed back then. He doesn't listen to a damn word I say. Who wants a player like that? A big headed un-coachable player. His ego alone fills that gym and I won't tolerate him tearing down what I work so hard to build. So as of now, yes he is off the team. Maybe if he is willing to practice with us and become a team player. Then he could have a spot back on the team."

Nathan said.

"Is this about me wanting to be friends?"

Joy asked.

"Wow, has it really come down to that? Joy our relationship doesn't affect my decision about Elijah."

Nathan said.

"I knew I shouldn't have even crossed the line with you."

Joy replied.

"What is that supposed to mean? If there's something you want to tell me, please feel free to do so."

Nathan spat.

"It's just so damn coincidental that the moment I say friends. all of a sudden my son is off the team. You know what I see you are the same ole jealous, spoiled, conniving son of a bitch!"

Joy yelled.

"Jealous! Wow so now I'm jealous of your son. I went pro I lived my dream. What do I have to be jealous about. Conniving, really that's how you feel that's what you think of me?"

Nathan said hurt to say the least.

"I should have known you of all people couldn't change."

Joy said.

"You know what then Joy obviously, you don't know me. You right, huge mistake thinking we could pick up where we left off. You go your way and I will go mine. As far as your son goes when he is ready to be a team player he can be back on the team."

Nathan said before getting in his truck.

The words Joy said cut him deeper than any object could. Heading to her car she got in and sped off. Nathan fought the urge to get a drink. Instead he headed to the gym to blow off some steam.

Surprised to see a call from his ex-wife. Nathan answered on the first ring.

"Happy anniversary even though we're no longer together."

She said.

"Happy anniversary to you too."

Nathan said.

"What are you up to today?"

Melanie asked.

"At the gym, I didn't know what else to do."

Nathan chuckled.

"Figures, you would be keeping yourself up. Meanwhile, I'm sipping wine and eating chocolates."

She laughed.

"Sounds like you're having fun over there."

Nathan replied.

"Hardly but I guess I'll let you get back to working out."

She said.

"How about you go get dressed and I get dressed up and we go somewhere?"

Nathan suggested.

"Are you serious?"

Melanie asked.

"Yeah let's go out and do something fun."

He said.

"Okay give me an hour to get ready. I will see you when you get here."

Melanie said before hanging up.

Nathan went home to get dressed. Taking a shower, he shaved and lined up his hair. Thinking of places to go he decided to take her out to Jackson, Mississippi. They could have dinner and go see a show.

Once he was dressed Nathan went to pick up a few things to pass time. After an hour passed, he was at his old house. Ringing the doorbell with a dozen of pink roses and a huge teddy bear. Along with her favorite chocolate candies. When Melanie answered the door, she was surprised.

"Nathan, you didn't have to get all of this."

She smiled.

"If you don't want it you know I can just get rid of it."

Nathan teased walking off.

"No of course I want them, don't play with me."

Melanie said.

"That's what I thought. You look beautiful, you ready to go?"

He asked.

"Yeah just let me put these flowers in some water."

She said.

Nathan waited on her until she was ready. He pulled out all the stops from opening her door to playing her favorite songs.

"I really miss this side of you. I miss us being happy like this."

Melanie said.

"Me too."

Nathan smiled as they rode along listening to the sounds of Jaheim. Melanie turned up the volume when "You Can Have Anything" began to play.

"Aww, I love this song remember when you sang it to me your freshman year. You took me to the park and we had a picnic with a spread made with two Popeyes' five dollar boxes."

Melanie laughed.

"Hey that's all I could afford but I promised to give you the world."

Nathan said.

"You gave me more, it was never about money or fame. We have three precious little angels. All I ever wanted was your love."

Melanie said.

"I know and I'm sorry for hurting you Mel. You were perfect and I messed it all up. Thinking I was missing out on something. I lost my family, I lost my career, I even lost myself. Look at me Mel, I'm back in my hometown coaching some knuckle head high schoolers. They think once you go pro all the problems are solved. In reality, that's when more problems come. I just wish I could have a do over. Then maybe you wouldn't have been so disappointed in me."

Nathan said.

"I was hurt Nathan and it's been really hard. The kids miss you and every single day I have to hear why does daddy live so far? Or why come daddy don't love us anymore. I really just wished the divorce never happened. Maybe things could have worked out had I been more willing to try."

Melanie said.

"You had every right to be upset. It wasn't like I messed up one time. So this is all on me, I just hope we can be at a place where I can be around more. Leaving the kids afterwards each and every visit breaks my heart."

Nathan said.

"Well for now let's enjoy this moment. The past is the past and this is now."

She smiled.

Pulling up to a sushi bar and grill. Nathan and Melanie laughed, ate and talked. It felt like old times until the night came closer to the end.

The drive back to the house Melanie fell asleep on Nathan's shoulder. As good as it felt all he could think about was Joy. He knew they were on bad terms for the moment. He just couldn't shake the feelings off, the night they stayed together. Joy could pretend that it meant nothing.

Nathan saw it as being much more but what good was that if the feeling wasn't mutual. He just had to accept that Joy didn't feel the way he felt about her. Looking over at Melanie as she slept. She was everything any man could want in a woman. Maybe this is where he belonged.

Parking in the driveway of the house, Nathan shut the truck off. Gently tapping Melanie, he tried to wake her.

"I'm sorry for falling asleep on you."

she said yawning.

"It's fine, let me walk you to the door."

Nathan said getting out the truck to open her door for her.

"Thanks for taking me out."

Melanie smiled once they were at the front door.

"Thanks for allowing me."

Nathan replied.

"Would you like to come in for a cup of coffee?"

she said seductively.

"Uh…yea…Yeah…I mean yes."

Nathan said nervous and excited all at the same time.

"I have never seen you blush like this. For someone who is known to always be smooth."

Melanie laughed.

"Hey that's not fair, I was caught off guard."

Nathan replied with a smile.

"As much as I want you to make love to me. I need to be sure if this is what I really want. What happens after sex, do we just go back to co-parenting. Or are we going to give it another shot."

Melanie said.

""So I'm guessing no coffee then."

Nathan sighed.

"Not tonight, I don't want to make any decisions off of my emotions. Let's take our time and go from there."

She said.

"I can respect that, is it okay if I see the girls tomorrow?"

Nathan asked.

"Yeah sure, just call me before you come and I can have them ready. Tonight, they are over Marie's for a slumber party."

She said.

"Okay then, I will call you tomorrow. Guess this is goodnight then."

Nathan said.

"Guess it is."

She said unlocking the door and stepping inside.

"Sure you don't want any coffee?"

Nathan said stepping to her.

Melanie was trying hard to put up a fight but the way her body was reacting to his touch. This was a losing battle on her part.

"I... I don't think that's a good idea."

She struggled with her words.

"Somebody's not as smooth as they used to be either""

Nathan smiled.

"Funny, I could have sworn I handled that well."

She replied with a smirk.

"How so?"

Nathan asked pressing his lips against her neck. Melanie ran her hands down his chest. Slowly making her way down his washboard. Stopping at the bulge in his pants, Melanie looked into his eyes.

"Because I'm the queen of tease, Goodnight."

Melanie said before shutting the door on him.

"Damn!"

Nathan said adjusting himself and heading to his truck.

Chapter Five

Jasmine

"Epiphany"

"I can't believe his ass!"

Joy spat as she stormed in the house and tossed her keys on the kitchen counter.

"Who?"

Jasmine said looking at her sister as if she lost her mind.

"Nathan that's who!"

Joy said as she paced back and forth ranting under her breath.

"Um did I miss something? Just a New York minute ago, you two were playing hide and go get it pornhub style. Now you up in here like you caught him cheating with a white girl. Oh snap! he cheating ain't he? Is she a blonde? Hell, at least it's a woman. Wait it is a woman who he cheating with right?"

Jasmine asked while closing the refrigerator door.

"No Jas damn! Nathan kicked Elijah off the basketball team. Maybe if I hadn't taken it there with him. Then none of this would have happened. I mean what other explanation is there for him to do this shit."

Joy said having a seat across from her on the breakfast bar.

"Damn J, I told you it was gone be hell. You gave him a taste and now he's a certified Joy nookie fiend. Now what yo ass gone do because I tried to warn you."

Jasmine said trying to keep from laughing.

"Jas I really could slap you right about now. This is serious, what am I going to do? Elijah could lose a chance to get a full ride. I don;t want to be the mother that always fucks up."

Joy said.

"Look okay, we could just blackmail him. Find some dirt on him, threaten to use it in exchange to get nephew back on the team."

Jasmine said while mixing up her a bottle water and Lipton peach tea single.

"How the hell am I going to do that Jas? Yo ass watch too much TV, that crap will never work."

Joy said.

"If you go stake him out see what he up to. I'm sure everybody in this town has some dirt on them."

Jasmine said sipping her drink.

"Maybe I should ask Charlene for help."

Joy said.

"You just want to go see her so yo ass can try to fuck."

Jasmine replied rolling her eyes.

"Everything isn't about sex Jas, plus I could use real advice."

Joy said grabbing her keys and heading for the door.

"Oh ok, that's fine just ignore your baby sister!"

Jas yelled and went back to her drink.

Just as she was about to watch new episodes of Bad Girls Club, her phone rang and David was calling again. Not wanting to talk she sent him to voicemail.

"Let's see which one of these bitches get kicked out the house first."

Jasmine said grabbing the remote and laying down on the sofa. Twenty minutes in and Jasmine was yelling at the TV.

"Oh hell no, she done lost her damn mind! Whoop that bitch ass for eating up all yo shit! See that's why I don't do reality because it couldn't have been me baby! I would have knocked all train of thought out of her."

Jasmine spat.

There was a knock on the door and she hit pause on the remote.

"Now who is this interrupting my chill time damn?" Jasmine mumbled getting up.

When she opened the door David was standing there.

"You have got to be kidding me!"

Jasmine said pissed off.

"I know I shouldn't have just popped up on you like this. Jasmine I needed to see you, please just talk to me. You haven't been home or answering your phone."

He said.

"That's because I am still in shock! I walked in on my husband being fucked by another man! Excuse me for not wanting to be bothered but since you here and wanna talk. Tell me David did you enjoy it? Oh, and just so we are clear I'm referring to the fucked in the ass part."

Jasmine spat awaiting his response.

"Jasmine no! Can you be reasonable for once please."

David said.

"Is that a no you didn't enjoy it? Had I not walked in you probably wouldn't have stopped it. Get the fuck out of here David you're gay and I was just a cover up."

Jasmine said feeling herself about to snap out.

"I'm not gay, I was curious like I told you. It was only one time and I am done with that."

He said.

"Yeah right and Rupaul is marrying a woman. You really think I am dumb enough to believe that you're straight? After being fucked in the ass by a big Deebo looking ass nigga. Read my lips David fuck you and have a nice life."

Jasmine said trying to shut the door on him.

"Wait Jas please, I love you and I can explain everything please. I'll tell you the truth about everything. For a while I thought I was gay. I needed to know if I slept with a man and liked it I would know for sure. I didn't have an erection at all."

David said.

"Spare me the homeboy on homeboy details. You gay for taking it that far for one. If you weren't, that shit wouldn't have went the way it did."

Jasmine said.

"I know and I am ashamed to even have done it. All I want is you Jasmine and I'm sorry for putting you through this."

David said.

"David please, you only sorry that you got caught. I want nothing to do with you. We can sell the house I want a divorce. It's over so just accept it and move on. David if you come back over here again, I will place a restraining order against you. Stop calling me, don't text me, leave me the fuck alone."

Jasmine spat before slamming the door in his face.

Sitting back down on the couch she pressed play on her show. Picking up her cell she blocked David in her phone. All the excuses in the world couldn't help his ass. Jasmine just needed space and time to plan her next moves. Trying to get back into her show. There was another knock at the door.

"See that's exactly why you can't date law enforcement. They think they Drew Peterson, the untouchables."

Jasmine fussed on the way to open the door.

Snatching it open Jasmine went off.

"Look it's over and I told yo ass to leave!"

Jasmine yelled.

"Hey did I catch you at a bad time?"

The guy replied who clearly wasn't David.

"Oh my God I am so sorry my ex was just here and wow. I must seem real crazy, huh?"

Jasmine asked with an embarrassing laugh.

"Not at all, you seem strong minded obviously beautiful and has zero tolerance for bs."

He said.

Jasmine smiled and peeped that this stranger before was not too bad looking.

He was not her usual dark chocolate but as a light skin brother he was still fine. Broad shoulders, low crisp lined Caesar, hazel eyes, chiseled chest, and tall!

Although David was an inch taller, they were still sort of eye level. It was just something Jasmine loved about a tall man.

"I know you must be wondering who I am. My name is Jalen and I just moved here from L.A. my mother owns the house next door. She hasn't been her best, so I moved back to care for her. I don't believe in nursing homes. So, I was trying to get information about a in home nurse. I have no reception on my cell here. My mother doesn't have long distance. So I am pretty much at a stand-still."

He said with a smile.

The more Jasmine looked at this stranger, the more she begin to imagine things she would do to him. He was a dangerous kind of sexy. Normally pretty boys were not her cup of tea. However, Jalen had this type of ruggedness to him.

"Your arms are really nice you must work out a lot."

Jasmine said.

"Yeah fitness is required with my line of work."

Jalen replied.

"I'm sorry, you needed to use the phone. Please come on in, I can get you a phone book if you like?"

Jasmine stepped aside letting him in.

"This is nice, looks much different than the way Mrs. Anderson used to have the place."

Jalen replied.

"You grew up here in Canton?"

Jasmine asked.

"Yeah, up until my sophomore year of high school. Then my pop and mom split, my sister stayed with my mom. I went with my dad to keep the confusion down. The divorce took a toll on both me and my sister."

Jalen replied.

"Oh I bet, so sorry to hear that. I grew up here too, I might know your sister, who is she?"

Jasmine asked.

"Janice Smith she lives out in Jackson but she comes here every day."

He said.

"Janice Matthews is your sister, that's my best friend. She was my maid of honor, she did say her mother was sick. I don't remember her having a brother back in the day. There was a big ole fat boy that used to be at her house. Maybe he was her cousin or something."

Jasmine said.

"I doubt it, I was her ole fat brother."

He said.

"I'm so sorry that was rude of me. I meant to say chunky, me and my big mouth. I didn't mean anything by it."

Jasmine said handing him the phone.

"Its fine, I got bullied and called far more worse. It's the past and it doesn't really bother me now."

Jalen replied.

"You look great though, I mean you lost the weight well."

Jasmine said nervously.

"Thanks," he said while dialing some numbers on the house phone.

"Looks like my sister is not picking up."

He said.

"Let me try to call her maybe I can get her."

Jasmine said grabbing her cellphone.

She waited until Janice voice came through the speaker.

"Hey boo, you feeling better today?"

Janice asked.

"Yeah, much better. Hey your brother Jalen is at my sister's house. He was trying to reach you."

Jasmine said.

"Who Jalen?"

Janice asked.

"Yeah you know Joy bought the house next door to your mother's house."

Jasmine said.

"Oh yeah, okay is he still there?"

Janice asked.

"Yeah, just a second."

Jasmine said handing Jalen her cellphone.

"Hello? Momma doesn't have long distance and my phone has no signal here. I been trying to get her a nurse all morning. All the locations are long distance."

He said.

Jasmine tried to be productive and clean up so it wouldn't appear that she was eavesdropping.

"I'm going to check a few places out before I decide on a nurse. Still waiting on my transfer before I can work again. Yeah, I know and dad supposed to send some money to help mom out. He is still our father Janice, it was the past. I love you too sis yeah see you later."

Jalen said before ending the call.

"Hey thanks for letting me use your phone. I think I might have to switch companies since I'm back down south."

Jalen said handing Jasmine her phone.

"Yeah my sister moved from D.C. and she switched services too."

Jasmine said.

"Your sister used to be the local Lisa Leslie ,she still ball?"
Jalen asked.
"Not really, she's more of a business exec type now."
Jasmine replied.
"It was nice talking to you thanks again."
Jalen said heading for the door.
"Hey, if you ever need anything I don't be busy so I could help."
Jasmine said.
"Thanks that really means a lot."
He smiled.
"Anytime, oh and sorry again about earlier."
Jasmine went on.
"Its fine you take care."
Jalen said before leaving.
Jasmine peeped out of the window as he walked next door.
"Sweet Jesus, that man is fine!"
She said fanning herself.
As long as her and Janice been friends, she never thought twice about her best friend's brother. He was always nice but Jasmine always had a boyfriend in high school.
"It always be the fat ones that glow up."
Jasmine said.
Elijah walked in from school and anyone could see how frustrated he was.
"Hey nephew, care to talk about what's got you in a funk?"
Jasmine asked.
"Hey auntie Jas, it's just I got kicked off the team by momma friend. I swear I don't like that dude he thinks cause he messed up in the league, everybody else gone follow in his footsteps."
Elijah spat.
"I am sure your mom is going to fix it. They go way back, maybe this whole thing is a misunderstanding."
Jasmine told him.
"I hope so because I have enough to worry about."
He replied.
"Where is Juniqua, anyways?"
Jasmine asked.

"Staying with her cousin I guess she call herself being mad at me."

he said.

"Go check on her still, she supposed to be working at my shop."

Jasmine told him.

"I will, when I get done studying."

He said.

"I'm going to step out, hit my line if you need something!"

Jasmine said grabbing her purse and keys.

Jalen was underneath his hood of his jeep. Jasmine decided to head over to invite him out to dinner.

"Hey, I was about to go grab something to eat, you hungry?"

She asked.

"Yeah sure, let me just make sure my mom doesn't need anything."

He said going into the house.

Jasmine stood and waited until he came back out.

"Okay so are we all ready to go? "

Jalen asked.

"Are we taking your car or mine?"

Jasmine asked as he put the hood down.

"We can take mine, I just put some oil in it."

Jalen said.

Jasmine climbed in on the passenger side. Jalen got behind the wheel and buckled up. Trying to decide where to eat they decided to go for some crawfish.

"I haven't had any in a while, these are really good."

Jalen replied.

"We should go to Gulfport, they have the best crawfish and gumbo."

Jasmine told him.

"It's crazy how I'm eating with my old crush. Man, back then I dreamed of asking you out on a date. When I did get the courage to ask, you already had a boyfriend."

Jalen said remembering back.

"I would have considered taking you up on your offer but just as a friend."

Jasmine replied.

"So, you mean to tell me, back in high school you would have went out on a date with me? Now that, I just don't believe."

Jalen laughed.

"I mean yes, as a friend we could of had dinner or lunch. Just like we are now, I'm not that shallow. Besides, regardless of how you looked I still wouldn't date you. For the mere fact that you're two years younger than me plus your sister and I are like sisters."

Jasmine said.

"So we family now. I mean if you claim my sis then that makes us kin too."

He said.

"Oh for sho! We family now, since you paying for these crab legs I'm about to order."

Jasmine said getting the waiter's attention.

"You a trip but, I see now that we gone have some problems. You can't be saying we kin and not hook me up. I know you got a friend or someone I can ask out."

He said while taking a sip of his drink.

"I may know a few ladies but they not for you. I mean if that's what you want then hey go for it. In my opinion I think you can do better than the chicks I know from Canton."

Jasmine said.

"I ain't looking to find someone perfect. Just somebody to kick it with, you know."

Jalen told her.

"You hardly need to kick it, in fact when you gone settle down anyway?"

Jasmine asked.

"Can't say, maybe when the right woman comes along. Until then I'm just trying to kick it."

He said.

"I guess, so was there anyone special back in California or was you kicking it there too?"

Jasmine asked.

"There was, she was an inspiring actress. She felt like me moving back here would complicate our relationship. I only have one mother so it is what it is. We went our separate ways because there ain't no woman more important than my mother."

He said.

"I heard that, she must have never really loved you then. Something like your situation is understandable. How can you get upset about a man caring for his mother? I don't even know the chick and I don't like her already."

Jasmine said with a frown.

"Neither did my sister, I guess there was no love lost there." Jalen laughed.

"Jalen, can I ask you something? Don't get upset. I just want a man's perspective to make sure I am not completely insane."

Jasmine said.

"Okay, I hope whatever it is doesn't affect our new-found friendship."

Jalen said nervously.

"It's a personal issue and as a man I wanted your opinion. I recently got married and it was all good until the passing of my father."

Jasmine went on to tell him.

"Sorry to hear that about your father."

Jalen said sincerely.

"Thanks, so my husband is a homicide detective, sometimes he gets called in. I understand that sometimes his job keeps him away. The day of my father's funeral, my husband was gone. He came to the funeral and at the cemetery he must have left. Our bank account sends text alerts whenever a purchase is made. So my phone went off and the email showed the name of a hotel. We live in Jackson, so it made no sense for him to get a room here in Canton. So, the first thing came to mind was he's seeing someone. I get to the hotel and I see my husband in the shower. he wasn't alone though and he wasn't showering."

Jasmine said.

"Damn another woman sorry to hear that Jasmine."

Jalen said.

"It was another man actually."

Jasmine replied.

Jalen went into a coughing fit, a look of horror on his face.

"Are you okay?"

Jasmine asked as he choked on his food.

"Nah, I'm good just caught me by surprise. You said it was a man, like a man-man?"

Jalen asked wide eyed in shock.

"Yes and he said he was curious about being with a man. Are all guys curious about other men sexually?"

Jasmine asked.

"Hell nah!"

Jalen said.

"I figured he was lying to me."

Jasmine sighed.

"Look obviously, he shouldn't have married you. If he had those kinds of feelings. He most definitely gay for that shit. The question is, what are you going to do?"

Jalen asked.

"Do I really have a choice now. I can't be married to a gay man. This is so fucked up like it's one thing if he cheated with a woman. Hell, I could compete but a man, no fucking way. I already have divorce papers, I was just thinking of my next moves. He won't stop calling even came by before you did. I had to block him on my phone. To top it all off I'm pregnant and I don't even know if I want him to know. What would I tell my child, that he or she father is gay. Do I even want my child to have two fathers? Hell, three fathers if I ever decide to date again. How crazy does that sound for a child to have that many fathers. Sound like I'm a hoe and I was married."

Jasmine laughed.

"Listen don't beat yourself up and more importantly stop over thinking. Take it one day at a time and if you need anything I'm only a phone call away. Well that is when I change phone service providers."

Jalen smiled.

"Thank you, Jalen that is so sweet of you."

Jasmine said feeling a lot better.

"I could use someone to help me with finding a home healthcare provider for my mom?"

Jalen asked her.

"Sure, we can check out a few places out in Jackson."

She said.

After lunch, they rode to see a few healthcare companies. So far, they struggled to find one that Jalen's mom's insurance covered. He would have to pay out of pocket.

"Okay, so what's the budget price you can cover for any of these services?"

Jasmine asked taking out a notebook and pen to jot down Jalen's finances.

"I have a little bit of savings and just waiting on my transfer to the Jackson fire department. It should be another week or so. Until then I draw unemployment about three hundred a week."

He said.

"Wow so you are a fire fighter?"

Jasmine asked.

"Yeah I know it's kind of corny to be what you wanted to be as a child."

He smiled.

"No, actually its admirable I own a flower shop. I love flowers, my mother did too before she passed."

Jasmine replied.

"Sorry about your mom, you been through a lot. Here I am putting my problems on you. I can't thank you enough for everything you've done to help me."

He said.

"No, it's not a problem my siblings and I, we keep each other strong. Trust me I have handled plenty more than this."

She said as they pulled up to his mother's house.

"It's pouring down pretty bad now, you want me to run and go get you a umbrella?

He asked.

"A little rain never hurt nobody."

she said.

"The Jasmine I remember used to be afraid of thunderstorms. You ain't gotta front for me girl.'

Jalen teased.

"That was then. I have grown now, in fact I can show you better than I can tell you."

Jasmine said opening her door.

The wind blew as the rain poured down continuously. The loud thunder caused Jasmine to jump and shut her door. She hit the locks and held on to Jalen's arm.

"Oh yeah you changed a lot alright. You went from long screams to short ones."

He laughed.

"Shut up, how are we supposed to get inside because I am not going out there."

She said.

"I thought a little rain never hurt anybody."

He mocked.

"Ugh, that was before it started lightning and thundering."

Jasmine said.

"It will pass, in the meantime let's try to stay warm."

Jalen said turning on some heat.

"This is slick, romantic with the rain storm and being stuck in the car together. If only we had some music."

Jasmine said.

"The good thing about music is as long as you got a voice you have music."

He smiled.

"Oh no, I suck at singing. Joy is the singer in my family."

Jasmine laughed.

"Okay then I will sing, how about that?"

He said.

"Oh Lord you sure you wanna do that?"

Jasmine asked.

Jalen shrugged and cleared his throat.

Jasmine was too busy laughing at him that when he begins singing she was taken aback.

"Open your heart and let me pour my loving inside of you, baby.

You make me feel like living and breathing again, I wanna touch you'

Don't saaaaaay, no

Say yessssss, your body's what I need."

Jasmine was so wrapped up in his soulful voice, she didn't bother to utter another word. Jalen's serenade to her was so intense. He leaned in and finished with a kiss. Jasmine closed her eyes, and the tingle up her spine ignited the spark between her thighs.

Unknowingly she moaned, enjoying the feel of his soft lips. Jalen didn't want this moment to end. He dreamed of kissing her for years. Here they were years later doing just what he envisioned.

"I love you!"

He told her in between slow sensual kisses.

Jasmine eyes fluttered open the moment she heard the words. Pulling away, Jasmine couldn't believe what had happened.

"Jalen, I think I should go."

She said as her heart raced.

Jasmine had never been kissed with so much passion before. So much that it scared her to feel what she was feeling.

"Wait Jas please don't go. I know I crossed the line but I have wanted you since the first time I laid eyes on you. Can't you see that this couldn't have been a coincident. Me moving back here and running into you."

He said.

"Jalen, I'm married and this is wrong. Regardless of my situation this isn't right. This was a mistake I shouldn't have asked you to lunch."

Jasmine said unable to look at him in fear of wanting to kiss him again.

"Don't say that Jas, what I feel isn't a mistake. You gotta feel it too just stop and hear me out for a second."

He pleaded.

"No I have to go and you should go too."

Jasmine said unlocking the car door and getting out into the rain. Jalen hoped out after her calling her name.

"Jasmine please!"

He yelled out but Jasmine kept it moving until she was on the porch of her sister's house. Soaking wet she fumbled in her purse for her set of house keys.

"Jasmine can you just hear me out."

Jalen said walking up onto the porch.

"Could you just stop it? It was a mistake now leave please."

Jasmine yelled.

"I'm sorry, alright I'll go."

Jalen said turning to leave.

Once in the house, Jasmine broke down crying. Confused if it was her emotions getting the best of her, she couldn't understand why she was feeling like this. Here she was married and pregnant. Yet she felt a deeper connection with another man who she hadn't seen in years rather than with the man she married.

"Jas what's wrong? You okay, did David do something to you?"

Joy asked worried rushing to her sister's side.

"I don't know what is going on anymore."

Jasmine cried.

"Slow down sweetie, calm down take a deep breath. Now tell me what happened?"

Joy asked.

"I just need to sleep that's all."

She said not ready to tell her sister everything.

"Okay then I will draw you a warm bath. Get you some rest we can talk whenever you're ready."

Joy told her.

Jasmine took a bubble bath and thought about everything that happened with Jalen. Convincing herself that it was her hormones that caused this.

She just needed to keep away from both David and Jalen. How she was going to do that was the hard part. Until then she planned on avoiding both.

Chapter Six

Carmen

"Like Old Times"

"Hey there, go my baby girl!"

Carmen's father greeted her. Being back in North Carolina brought back memories.

"Hey daddy!"

She replied giving him the biggest hug. Loading up in his '86 Brougham they headed to the house. Al Green's "Let's Stay Together" played as they cruised through the streets of Charlotte. Heading towards the outskirts in the country.

"So how's my baby girl been?"

Her father asked.

"I been good daddy just got tired of being away for so long. I hope it's alright if me and the kids stay until I get on my feet."

She said.

"Sho'nuff baby girl, that ain't t no problem. What happened to Jackson he not working?"

Her father questioned.

"He and I just needed to be apart. He was laid off and with him staying in his father's house, who just past he needed to get things together. It shouldn't take him long to get on his feet."

Carmen said.

"He could of came here with you and got a job down at the plant."

He said.

"He probably will, once he get everything settled with his father house. It's in the process of being renovated."

Carmen lied.

She couldn't bring herself to tell him that she was being beaten nearly every other day.

"Okay then, boy we got a house full of people that came to see you girl. Your momma done called up everybody. You know she know everybody in the state of North Carolina. We got catfish and spaghetti, plenty of room for the kids to play outside. Tomorrow I'm cleaning out my pit and bbq. Throw some ribs and chicken on the grill. Sit outside like old times, how you like the sound of that?"

He asked smiling.

"That sounds good I can't wait to taste some of you and momma's cooking."

Carmen said while closing her eyes.

She could almost taste the homemade southern soul food. Looking out into the field on the old gravel road. Carmen forgot all about how far in the country her family lived. The houses were coming into view. The little community was as big as two spins. Cars were lined up you would have thought it was a family reunion.

Once they parked, Carmen and the kids walked over towards the yard filled with nothing but family. Hugging everyone from cousins to uncles to aunties and close friends of the family. Carmen watched as the family laughed and had drinks.

Uncle Raymond especially, he was on his third beer as far as Carmen was counting. It wasn't no telling how many he had before she arrived. Cousin Pookie broke out the stereo equipment and played some blues. Uncle Raymond was the first one on the dance floor, drunk and all.

"Sooooooo you say yo sister saw me! Whew! Coming out the Holiday Inn."

Raymond sang loudly.

"Alright now Ray what you doing in that there hotel?"

Carmen's mother Gloria teased.

"And the woman I was with! Used to be yo very best friend. Well she must need glasses cause it sho wasn't me!"

Raymond sang.

Carmen laughed as they watched Raymond sing Tyrone Davis.

"Check it out, y'all look who done brought out the liquor!"

Cousin Pookie yelled out pointing to Roy.

Everyone knew Roy and Carmen used to be the country Will and Jada. Until they each went on to college and lost touch. Carmen went her way and he went his. Years later here they were like old times in the flesh.

"Roy, is that you? Boy you better give me a hug and come get you a plate!"

Gloria said excited to see him.

Carmen's mother tolerated Jackson but Roy was her favorite. Even at her and Jackson's wedding reception she mentioned Roy. Carmen watched as her mother put on a show.

"You know Carmen is back! I knew that proper city boy and her wouldn't last too long. I told that girl long before she married not to move too far away from home."

Gloria went on.

"Momma! Jackson isn't even from the city, he from Mississippi remember.

Carmen said.

"Still sound uppity."

She replied.

"Hey Carmen, I see you looking good. How you been? It's been a long time."

Roy smiled.

"I been fine Roy."

Carmen said.

"I can see that."

He smiled while eying her body.

Carmen didn't feel sexy or desirable at all. Self consciously she looked down. Roy noticed that Carmen wasn't the upbeat confident southern beauty she once was. Instead she displayed uncertainty and lacked hardly any confidence.

Being able to read body language. Roy also noticed how uncomfortable she was by the way she fidgeted with her clothes.

"You wanna go talk and catch up?"

Roy asked.

"That's fine."

She replied and followed his lead. Walking up the gravel rode they were both extremely quiet.

"So tell me how has life been treating you? I mean you look well, so you must be a big-time teacher in where was it again you moved to?"

Roy asked.

Carmen had forgot the entire reason why she moved away from home. She was supposed to be a teacher by now. Instead she was a miserable abused housewife. The tears began to fall at the thought of how much of her life she wasted.

"Hey now what's with the tears?"

Roy said.

"I'm sorry, it's just I didn't expect to end up back where I started at with nothing accomplished."

Carmen cried.

"You don't have to apologize about anything. It's never too late to follow your dreams Carmen. You're intelligent and you're ambitious. When you said, you were leaving for college, I had no doubts that you wouldn't do exactly what you said you would do."

He said.

"I can't even take care of my kids. I put so much into my marriage that I don't know who I am anymore."

Carmen said.

"Nothing is overnight, give yourself time to get back to being you."

Roy encouraged her.

"Thank you for not judging me."

Carmen smiled.

"Oh never, we go back, way back."

Roy said smiling.

"Dang, we walked a bit of a ways, didn't we?"

She said seeing how far they were away from the house. The cars looked tiny from where they stood.

"As long as we talking it won't seem far."

He assured her.

"This is the most I ever walked I know you noticed the weight gain.""

Carmen said putting her head down again.

"As long as you happy with the way you look, what anyone else thinks is irrelevant."

Roy said.

"I want to lose weight but with being depressed, it's just been too hard and I gave up on trying."

She replied.

"I can walk with you every morning. We can ride into the city for gym memberships."

He told her.

"I don't know when I would be able to pay you back."

She said.

"I didn't ask you to now did I?"

Roy asked.

"No but I wouldn't feel right not paying for my own membership."

She said.

"Anybody ever tell you how stubborn you are."

Roy teased.

She didn't reply, instead she enjoyed the peaceful walk in the country. Once they got back to the house it seemed as if more people had shown up. Carmen's kids were inside while the drinkers sipped outside.

Looking at the stars the night couldn't have been more perfect. Roy and she talked for hours on in. Finally deciding to call it a night she headed inside.

"Baby girl you got a minute for your old man?"

Her father asked.

"Sure daddy, what you need?"

She replied.

"Now I'm not one to meddle in your business but, from the looks between you and Roy."

He said.

"I know how it may look daddy but I can assure you we are just friends."

She said in her defense.

"I hear you just be considerate and mindful that you took a vow. As much as I don't believe in divorce. I rather you divorce than to move on to the next with unresolved issues with your past partner. I raised you right so I know you will do what's right."

He said.

"I will daddy you don't have to worry."

She assured him.

Heading to bed she gave his words some thought. She did share something with Roy tonight. Maybe she really was ready to move on from Jackson. Only time would tell for now, her focus was her kids and getting back to her dreams.

Carmen couldn't express how much she missed waking up to the smell of her mother's breakfast cooking on the stove. The kids were up and so was she. Roy sent her a good morning text. With a smile a mile wide, Carmen was like a love struck teen all over again. Starting off her morning she cleaned herself up for breakfast.

"You sure are cheery this morning."

Her mother replied as Carmen had a seat at the dining table.

"Can't I be in a good mood momma?"

Carmen smiled.

"Yes you can, but I wanna know who put you in that mood."

She smiled.

"Momma, nobody but you all. I miss being home and it feels good to be back."

She replied.

"We happy you home too baby."

Her mother said.

As if he read her mind, Roy sent Carmen another text. It read, "Thinking of you" along with a heart eyed emoji face. Unable to hide her smile she decided to text him back. After a few back and forth texts of nonstop flirting. Carmen had agreed to meet him for dinner.

Although she told her father there was nothing between her and Roy. Still she couldn't help but feel excited about being alone with him.

"Momma is Doreen's salon open today? Think I want her to give me a new look."

Carmen said.

"Yeah she's open every day 'cept Sunday. You want me to go with you, I usually go on Wednesday but today is fine."

She replied.

"Sounds good to me, you think daddy will be alright watching the kids? You know Doreen ain't exactly a timely stylist."

Carmen said.

"He will be fine, let me go get dressed."

Her mother said.

Doreen's salon was the place all the women gathered to get their hair slayed and hear the latest gossip.

"Y'all know Willie was caught sneaking over to Geraldine house last night. Said Francis followed him there and ended up kicking in that woman's door. I wish I had of been the bush or the mailbox to see that showdown!"

Doreen said as the shop erupted in laughter.

"That ain't nothing, Mr. Herbert was working late at the funeral home last week. You know my nephew works as a director. His mother said he told her husband that Lillian stayed late with him. Found her slip, up in the casket display room."

Another older woman said.

"That old fool, gone die trying to get some tail."

Doreen laughed.

"Hey ladies, look who is back home with us?"

Carmen's mother said as she walked in.

"Child I ain't seen you in so long how you been?"

Doreen hugged her.

"I've been alright good to see everybody."

Carmen smiled.

"Where's that fine tail husband of yours?"

Doreen asked.

"In Mississippi, his father passed away so his dealing with all of that."

Carmen said.

"Oh I'm sorry to hear that how long you back?"

She asked.

'For good I think, my husband and I aren't doing so well. We're taking this time apart to figure things out."

Carmen replied.

"Oh well is you thinking about working it out?"

Another lady asked.

"Maggie what difference does it make? That young man don't want you!"

Doreen said.

The ladies laughed and that took all the spotlight off of Carmen. Doreen could sense she didn't really feel comfortable answering all of those questions. She had a way of redirecting the conversations in the shop. Carmen was grateful that she did being in the hot seat was no fun.

The women talked about any and everything under the sun. By the time Carmen got under the dryer, she knew who had babies on the way and with whom. She knew who was cheating and how long it's been going on.

That was only the information from last week's low down. She was overwhelmed about what all was going on the beginning of this week. The town was small and full of all types of drama. Carmen and her mother went to head over to the supermarket afterwards.

The bbq that her father had planned for today was going to bring in a crowd. They bought all the ingredients they needed for the side dishes along with a few packs of meat. Carmen constantly checked her phone. As the time got closer to seven o'clock, the more excited she was to see Roy.

"Mom, I'm about to get dressed and catch up with an old friend. Roy offered to drive me into town to see my friend."

She lied.

Carmen didn't want her parents to get the wrong ideas. She just wanted tonight to be about having fun. Roy was outside at seven on the dot. Carmen dressed appropriate not to give off the wrong impression. Not too appealing, yet chic with a taste of sexy.

Roy ended up going to a club, it was reggae night. Carmen hadn't been out in so long without her kids and husband.

"This is nice, what made you choose this place?"

Carmen asked him.

"I remember reggae being your favorite music."

He smiled.

"I forgot all about that, haven't listen to any in years."

She replied.

"Well tonight we drink up and turn up."

He said.

"Okay I can do that."

She said with a smile.

They ordered drinks and grooved to the sounds of Jamaica's baddest dancehall music. Getting the courage to get on the dancefloor, Carmen danced and let the music take her far away.

Swaying her body to the beat, Roy grinded up against her. It wasn't until she looked into his eyes that she realized this had become something much more. Leaning in, Roy kissed her gently. Carmen kissed him back she didn't care what her parents thought or her friends.

This was a moment they both shared and she didn't want it to end. Roy was a complete gentleman the entire night. Driving back to his place they had a glass wine.

Roy showed her around his apartment. Heading in the kitchen, Roy made sure not to get caught as he poured up some drinks. Slipping a pill into her glass, with a quick stir he returned back into the living room. Carmen thanked him as she grabbed the glass.

"A toast to old friends rekindling a friendship."

Roy said.

Carmen toasted and sipped from her glass. The taste was unusual and she began to feel light headed. Seconds later she laid back on the couch. Before you knew it, she was out of it.

Roy smiled to himself as Carmen laid passed out. Undressing her he caressed her unconscious body. Not sure if he wanted to have unprotected sex with her right away.

Her cellphone went off and he saw that her parents were calling. Putting her clothes back on he struggled to get her to the bed. Tonight, he would let her sleep the affects of the drugs off.

As for next time, he had plans on having himself a good time. Roy became obsessed with drugging women and having sex with them. He tested out all types of date rape drugs. His favorite was this new muscle relaxer. It temporarily paralyzed you but you were still conscious.

That way they couldn't move or feel a thing but was very much aware what was happening. The look in their eyes always took him over the edge. He had done it a countless of times.

Roy didn't have his eyes set on her anymore. He just planned on getting her to trust him. Who he really wanted was her daughter. He had been with two underage girls and enjoyed the sex better.

Carmen was already coming on to him. It would be only a matter of time before he gets her to fully commit to him. The next few hours he watched as she slept. Going through her purse he found a picture of her daughter. Sliding his hand in his pants he begin to jerk off.

"I can't wait to be inside you."

He whispered while kissing the little girl's photo.

Once he erupted, he cleaned himself up and placed the picture back in her purse. Carmen woke up to Roy asleep on the other couch. Trying to remember what exactly happened. She called her parents to tell them she was on her way.

"Roy wake up I need to go home."

She said trying to wake him.

Roy smiled at her and pretended to be happy to see her face.

"You had a bit too much wine and was knocked out."

He said.

"I did, figures why I don't remember a thing."

Carmen replied embarrassed.

"I didn't know whether to wake you or not. You were sleeping so peacefully and seemed tired."

He said.

"I must have been, sorry for ruining the night I thought I was well rested."

She said.

"Don't be let's get you home and we can pick up where we left off another time."

He smiled.

Carmen kissed him and grabbed her purse.

The ride out to her parents was long. She much rather had spent the night with Roy. Had it not been for the fact she had three little faces waiting on her.

"I had a good time, thank you for treating me to a nice night."

She said.

"I just want to make you happy. I never stopped loving you Carmen."

He said looking into her eyes.

Carmen smiled and kissed him again before leaving. If she was unsure before she damn sure was clear on what she wanted now. Jackson had plenty of chances and Roy was just what she needed.

"Carmen where on earth have you been? Bringing yo behind in here in the wee hours of the morning. You had me and your daddy worried sick."

Her mother fussed.

"Sorry momma I had fell asleep and lost track of time."

Carmen replied.

"Now we not gone stand for all of this staying out all times of the night. You said you came back to get yourself together. Not party all times of the night. While me and your daddy take care of your churrin!"

Her mother went on.

"Momma I know and I'm sorry it won't happen again."

She replied ready to go to bed.

"Lock my door and hopefully now we can get some darn sleep."

She said heading into her bedroom.

Carmen knew now, why she moved so far away. Her parents where overprotective. They had ridiculous rules and was always worried about her. Peeping into the guestroom, both of her boys were sound asleep.

Carmen quietly closed the door and went to her bedroom. Her daughter slept peacefully in her bed. Carmen took off her shoes and climbed under the covers. This is where she belonged; with her babies.

Sleeping for a few hours the sunlight shined through the window blinds. Carmen placed a pillow over her face shielding her eyes from the sunlight. Feeling light headed, she slowly sat up in bed.

She hadn't drunk wine in years and plan on not drinking anytime soon. Her daughter was out of bed. The clock on the nightstand flashed eight oh one. Getting up she went to the bathroom to go pee.

Carmen seen a glance of herself and forgot to wrap her hair up. It was messed up on one side. Grabbing a comb, she tried to fix it but it didn't look the same as it had before.

Running some cold water in the sink, she washed her face. Sitting on the toilet relieving herself Carmen flipped through a magazine. One of the kids were knocking on the bathroom door.

"Momma come look, grandpa got us a puppy!"

One of her sons said excitedly.

"I'll be out in a sec sweetie."

She replied while wiping and flushing. Washing her hands, she headed in her room and slid on her house slippers. The kids were all outside as she stepped out on the steps. Her father was leaning on the back of his pick-up truck in his work overalls.

"Mommy we naming him King."

Her youngest son smiled showing a toothless smile.

The puppy looked so cute and she remembered when her daddy got her a puppy around the age of seven. She named her Lilac and the two were inseparable. She was hit by a car when Carmen was around fourteen.

Carmen cried and grieved for days until her father told her good things never die. She could remember her daddy always being there when she needed him most. Which is why she felt bad for worrying him last night. Heading over to her father she asked if he had a minute to talk.

"Speak your peace child."

He said while cleaning underneath his fingernails with a switchblade. A habit her father had whenever he was deep in thought.

"Daddy I'm sorry about last night. I shouldn't have worried you and momma like that. It won't happen again and I hope you can forgive me."

She said.

"Never can stay upset over little things. You just make sure you are doing what will benefit those three young ones. You're a mother first, above all things. You are also my child and I love you. Which is why I am hard on you. Carmen you're smart like your mother. Can be anything you wish to be in this lil ole world. I just hope you don't let yourself get in the way of you achieving your greatness. Now it's up to you not to do what you always wanted. There's no time like the present baby girl. When you get off your behind and work at it. You'll see that it was all worth it."

He smiled.

"Yes sir, I love you daddy."

Carmen hugged and kissed her father's cheek.

"Love you too baby, I gotta get on to work. Make sho you think about what I said now you here."

He smiled getting in his truck.

"Bye granddad see you when you get home!"

The kids each said hugging him.

Carmen knew exactly what her father meant. He wanted her to finish school and be the teacher she always wanted to be. That's all she talked about as a child. She had dreams of becoming a well-known school teacher.

She wanted to be like Mr. Clark from the Lean On Me movie. To affect kids' lives the way he did. Teach them and guide them in the right direction.

Waving to her father as he drove off he honked his horn. Carmen was ready to get back to her game plan. Going back inside the house her mother was fixing herself some coffee.

"Morning momma."

Carmen said sitting down at the table.

"Morning baby, you want coffee?"

She asked.

"Sure, daddy and I talked I think I'm ready to go back to school."

Carmen told her.

"Well that's more like the child I raised.""

Her mother smiled.

"Finally going to be the teacher I always wanted to be."

Carmen smiled.

"I am proud of you, always have been. Don't get me wrong I know your young and got yo own life to live. Remember that you're still a married woman. You can't carry on as such you either gone fix your marriage or leave it, you here?"

She said.

"Yes ma'am."

Carmen replied.

The two sipped coffee and talked like old times. This is what she missed most. To be surrounded by people that supports and believes in her. This was home and with the love and support Carmen could fulfill her dreams.

Chapter Seven

Elijah

"Problems"

The walls inside the apartment shook as Ugly God's hit song "Water" bumped. Elijah was dressed down in Lacoste. With the brand new Space Jam black and white Jordan's on his feet. All eyes were on him as he and his friend Flex hit the dance floor.

Elijah danced with a few girls until he spotted Juniqua's cousin in the party. Walking up to him, she smiled in his face.

"Dang E, you act like you can't speak."

She smiled.

"Sup Khia, what y'all on?"

He asked.

"Nun just here to turn up, what you on?"

She asked.

"Same ish, you sauced I see tho."

Elijah complimented.

"Yup, you dripping I see you."

She flirted.

Not knowing how she was gone take it. Elijah decided to dance up on Juniqua's cousin. Gripping her waist, she twerked on him. The two headed into the bathroom together.

"What you on man for real?"

Khia asked.

"What you mean bruh, you act like you feeling me?"

He replied.

"I mean I am but you got a whole baby on the way with my cousin."

She said.

"Maaan you know that ain't my baby. She been with how many niggas. Yeah okay, exactly and you know since I'm balling she trying to catch fade."

Elijah said.

"You right, but ion know she still might feel some type of way."

Khia said.

"Man, no she ain't yo she didn't even know my name. Now come on we both know that's thotty as hell."

He laughed.

"Don't say that, but at least let me tell her."

Khia said.

"Tell her what, ain't shit to tell bruh we viben."

He told her.

Elijah's friend Flex started knocking on the bathroom door.

"Aye bro, yo baby momma up in here."

Flex said.

"See here we go, now she gone be on that bull."

Khia said.

Elijah walked out the bathroom and walked back into the party. He purposely ignored Juniqua and left out the party.

"So that's what we on, you gone fuck my cousin Elijah?"

Juniqua spat.

"Man we not together, that's not my baby!"

Elijah shrugged.

"Do whatever, I don't even care anymore."

Juniqua spat tearing up.

Watching her go into a different project apartment. Five minutes later Juniqua walked out with her things.

"Where you going?""

He yelled out to her.

She kept right on walking up the street.

"Juicy, man I didn't sleep wit her, you hear me?"

Elijah said running up behind her.

Grabbing her from behind, Elijah tried talking to her.

"That's messed up, how you just gone get with my cousin. I would never do no shit like that to you. Let me go Elijah, just move, go be with her."

Juniqua said.

"Where you gone go its late and its gone be cold."

Elijah said.

"I can stay in a shelter. Why you even care? You should be on yo way to fuck my cousin."

She spat.

"Man I should slap the shit out of you for saying that dumb shit. Quit being stubborn and just come back to the crib with me."

He told her.

"Why would I stay with you? Get the fuck off of me!"

She yelled.

"Fuck it then I'm out."

Elijah said letting her go and heading home. Halfway home he sent her a text.

*(You straight)- **Elijah 10:56 p.m.***

*(Yup)- **Juicy 10:57 p.m.***

*(Alright bruh)- **Elijah 10:58 p.m.***

Missed called-11:01 p.m.

Missed called-11:01 p.m.

Missed called-11:02 p.m.

(Gnite then)- *Elijah 11:04 p.m.*

(Y you call'n me 4)-**Juicy 11:08 *p.m.***

(Nvm bruh)- *Elijah 11:10 p.m.*

Incoming call from-Juicy

Elijah debated whether to send her to voicemail or not. He was really beginning to dislike Juniqua.

"What man?"

Elijah answered her call.

"You call?"

She said being extra petty.

"Nah, I hit you up by accident bruh."

He spat.

"Whatever, what do you want I'm about to hang up."

She said.

"Nun go head."

He told her.

"Well I'm on my way back to Jackson. My aunt taking me to live with my mother. You don't have to worry about me hitting you up again."

She said.

"That's cool then if that'' how you want it. I still want a DNA test done. If it's mine, I can't have random niggas around my baby. We all know how you get down."

Elijah said to purposely hurt her.

"I was waiting on you to degrade me. You do it so much it doesn't even bother me. If that's how you feel then fine. No reason for you to call me until after the baby comes. I don't have a problem getting a paternity test."

She said.

"Cool cause my girl been wanting to get this shit over with."

He said.

"Bye Elijah."

She said before hanging up.

Heading in the house, Joy was on the couch wide awake.

"So you think you can walk in this house when you feel like it? Elijah don't play yourself baby, I will knock yo ass into the next generation. Don't be walking in my house late as hell. Like yo ungrateful ass pay rent! Lock my door and get the fuck out my sight, before I reach out and touch you like a pastor. Move nigga!"

Joy said as calm but as serious as a heart attack.

Elijah quickly locked the door and headed to his room. He wanted to argue his side of walking in late. Seeing how serious she looked, the best idea was for him to keep it pushing.

Joy looked fifty shades of crazy and Elijah was not trying to be the first victim of her wrath. Changing clothes, he did a few snaps to Riley. Who was ignoring him still, she had been flaunting new I'm single pics all over social media.

Her Instagram photos were the most hurtful ones. Elijah could only imagine how many niggas was in her dm. He forgot he followed Juniqua on Snapchat too. She had snapped a crying emoji along with a broken heart. As tough as she acted, she was hurt by his words.

Trying to call her back she didn't answer. Deciding to leave her alone, Elijah went to sleep instead. Around five that morning Elijah woke up to his mother turning on his room light.

"Get up, if you want to be on the team you going to work hard. I was pregnant with you and still ran two miles every morning!"

Joy spat.

"Ma I'm sleepy can we do it this weekend?"

Elijah whined.

"Son do you think Michael Jordan slept in how about LeBron or Steph Curry, Damian Lillard? All those players work hard, no slacking. I had a perfect freshman college season. All because I worked my ass off. Fifteen MVPs, 89% shooting from the field goal, a minimum of ten rebounds a game, seven assists and at least three steals. So until you can top my stats no sleeping in. You want to make it in the NBA then you gotta put in work."

Joy said.

"Momma those were college basketball stats I'm in high school."

Elijah said.

"Those are my high school stats, you not even ready for my college stats."

Joy said over her shoulder as she left the room.

"Lord, why couldn't I just have a regular mom."

Elijah said covering his face with a pillow. Ten minutes later, he was all dressed and ready to run.

"Okay since this is only day one we gone run a mile do some squats, jumps, pushups and work on your weak ass assists. Just because you can shoot don't mean you Curry. The one man show has to end if you want to be an all-around well player. You play as a team and you win as a team.""

Joy said.

"Yes ma'am."

He sighed not really wanting to hear all the speeches.

Joy notice his attitude and knew she had to break him. They began running their one mile. As much as Elijah was ready to go back to sleep he enjoyed the workout. Running back to the house Joy had him work on jumps.

Elijah was well over six one and could dunk already. Joy needed him to guard and work on steals as well as he could shoot.

"Your offense is good but offense is nothing up to a player with great defense. Players like Tim Duncan, Mutombo, Shaq, Kevin Garnet, they were assets. You have to defend as well as you shoot. Or you gone be in for a rude awakening. Let's work on squats and foot movement."

Joy said.

"Mom, I already know this stuff."

Elijah bragged.

"See, there's that big head swelling up again. Here I am sharing with you some great basketball tips. All you can say is ma I already know."

Joy mocked.

"It's because I do ma, I'm the best player in Canton high."

Elijah said.

"Was, and so was I but if you think you so nice on the court. Put yo money where yo mouth is. I bet you on a one on one to ten I can beat the brakes off of you."

Joy said grabbing a basketball.

"Ma quit playing now, you vs me. If you want to lose ok then."

Elijah shrugged.

"You can get the ball first, there's a court up the street. You lucky you don't have money to play or else I would take yo money too."

Joy said.

"Mom you bugging, I ain't going easy on you either."

"That's fine, neither am I, you gone take this ass whooping."

Joy said as they walked up the street.

Tossing him the ball, Joy explained to Elijah the rules that the ball is to be checked. Elijah checked her and it was on from there.

Trying to crossover on his mom, Elijah was finding it difficult. She was all over him and didn't miss a beat. Stealing the ball, Joy made it behind the three-point line.

"Like I said, what's offense without defense."

She said as she checked him the ball.

Joy smiled as Elijah took a stance of his version of defense. She did a quick left then spun right and finger rolled in a lay-up.

"What's that 2 zip, you better "D" up this ain't love and basketball. This yo mom and basketball and right now I'm embarrassed to say you my son with garbage ass defense arms and stance like that."

Joy spat.

Elijah was getting upset as he checked her the ball back.

"Oh you mad now, well good use that anger to play better."

Joy spat.

With a pump fade and Elijah jumping up to block. Joy waited for him to come down before dropping another three pointer. Elijah was frustrated now he was done with seeing her as his mom. He couldn't lose to an old lady that's just ridiculous.

"I thought you already knew defense son.? See that's yo problem you think you know everything. Isn't that the way you got kicked off the team. Show boating won't help you against a player with defense. You can't even keep up with me, talking about the NBA. Nigga please, college ball might be out of your league. Step up or choose another career. I'm not about to baby sit or sugar coat shit to you just because you my son. You get no mercy, I want you to play better than me. Be better than me, succeed better than me. I'm not just gone be one of those moms that discipline you. No, I'm out here at six in the morning because I care. I see how bad you want this and I want it just as bad for you. So play baby, show me that this is what you want."

Joy said.

"I do momma but everybody is riding me. I'm trying, coach kicked me off the team. I can't play in tomorrow's game. This baby stuff and Riley, it's too much."

Elijah said with tears in his eyes.

"That's why I'm here son, I'm gonna get you back on that team with hard work. More schools are going to see how well you improved. With the stuff I am about to teach, man there won't be any limits. You will be unstoppable but you have to humble yourself. Don't worry about a girl right now. Focus on school, ball and the baby. We get a test if it's yours you will be in that child's life. You not gone be a deadbeat I won't stand for it you hear me?"

Joy said.

"Yes ma'am. Ma can you teach me defense? Now you already know you gone win, no sense in finishing this game it's embarrassing."

He said.

"Aww getting yo ass whooped isn't fun, you was sleeping on me son."

Joy laughed.

"Here we go with the jokes."

He said.

"After school we can start practice, until then you need to shower and get ready for school."

Joy said walking back towards the house.

"Mom who taught you how to cross like that?"

Elijah asked walking beside her.

"Believe it or not, Nathan showed me."

She replied.

"I messed up big time, huh?"

Elijah said.

"You not the only one, I sort of said some harsh words to him. So you not the only one on his bad list."

She said.

"Well you know what, you gotta do better, fix it. Friends are important to have especially good ones."

He told her.

"Well look who is giving some good advice. I hear you I plan on reaching out to him soon."

Joy assured him.

"I think he likes you too momma you better cuff him quick. You not getting no younger, I'm just saying."

Elijah teased.

"Say what, I am in my prime, shoot I look good. But you really think I should? We been friends a long time."

She said.

"Me and Riley were friends first but I messed it all up trying to stunt."

He replied.

"I think deep down Juniqua is good for you. Not now but maybe later on in life when you both get your act together. That girl really does love you. Might not see her worth now, but she has some good in her. We all have a past and I think she's a good girl that's damaged. Like I was, it happens to the best of us."

Joy said.

"Ma Juniqua has too many secrets. She acts innocent, me and Riley gone work things out."

He said.

"Hey if that's what you want I'll be happy to meet her."

She said.

Juniqua wasn't home a good twenty-four hours and she already wished she had stayed in Canton. She had to clean up the entire house. Starting with the bedrooms and doing all the laundry. The few weeks she was gone. It was like the whole house fell apart.

Cleaning her room first, she had never been happier to see her bed. Even though the room was a total wreck. Hanging up all her clothes she made her bed and vacuumed the floor. Playing music on her phone she plugged in her ear buds.

Her brother's room was next to clean. It wasn't too bad but her little sister's room took her over an hour alone to clean. Toys were everywhere and so was candy wrappers, empty soda cans, chip bags and dirty dishes.

"This don't make no sense how nasty this damn house is."

Juniqua spat looking at the kitchen.

Dirty dishes were in the sink, on the stove, countertops, and kitchen table. Cleaning out the sink the foul smell of spoiled food and dirty dishes, caused her stomach to turn and gag. Searching for a clean dish rag every towel in the house was dirty.

"Oh my fucking God, are you kidding me!"

Juniqua said walking into the laundry room to see tons of dirty clothes all over the floor. Postponing the dishes, instead she started a load of laundry, swept the kitchen floor and mopped afterwards.

Opening all the windows letting in some fresh air, Juniqua boiled a small pot of fabaloso cleaning solution, to give the house a fresh smell. Once the washer stopped, she started another load. Throwing the wet clothes in the dryer and cleaning out the lint filter. Since she didn't have rags to clean the kitchen or bathroom. The living room got cleaned instead.

Looking at the time it was dang near one o'clock. Taking out a pack of chicken to thaw. Juniqua figured since she already was cleaning, she might as well cook too.

The first load of towels were dry. She washed three loads of dishes and put them all away. Bleached the bathroom tub, sink and toilet. A hot shower was calling her name.

Scrubbing herself down she changed clothes and finished the laundry. When her siblings started coming in from school. She cooked them each some Ramen noodles. All the way each liked them.

"Juicy momma said you moved out cause you having a baby."

Her younger sister Shanae said.

"You just do yo homework and stay out of my business." Juniqua said.

No sooner had she said that, her momma walked in along with her boyfriend.

"Y'all might as well go to your room and get out of my living room. Shawn going to watch TV, so move. Baby you hungry, I can cook you some chicken wings and mashed potatoes?"

She asked her boyfriend.

"Yeah whip that up baby."

He replied kicking back on the couch.

"What you in my kitchen for? Her momma spat.

"I cleaned the house and was gonna cook dinner." Juniqua said.

"Well I'm cooking that pack of chicken wings for me and Shawn. Y'all can eat something else."

She said.

"Everything else frozen and gone take forever to thaw." Juniqua said.

"Well cook some noodles, hell."

Her mother said.

"Never mind I ain't cooking."

Juniqua said leaving out the kitchen.

"If yo ass got a problem you can take ya black ass back to Canton! You living here is only temporarily ain't no baby coming in here. Better find you a job too, since you wanna act grown. I need two hundred dollars rent."

Her mom yelled.

Going in her room, Juniqua wished she could rewind her life. Here she was living in her mother's house. Where her unborn child was not even allowed to stay in. Elijah was either throwing up her past or yelling he wasn't the father. It was to the point where she contemplated ending life all together.

Her notification from Instagram indicated she had a DM. Opening the app she read the message. It was from shooterEballsohard. She didn't reply the last thing on her mind was a dude. Elijah started calling and she picked up on the fifth ring.

"So you gone act like you didn't get my DM?"

He said.

"Why you hitting me up don't you got a lil girlfriend now?" She said.

"Here we go, so I can't call you now?"

He said.

"Bye Elijah."

She hung up and listened to music.

Juniqua went on Facebook and saw that her cousin was making subliminal posts. Sneak dissin' was one of her biggest pet peeves. Wanting to be petty she decided not to. Remembering everything didn't deserve a reaction.

She had enough shit on her mind like, where was she going to live. In Mississippi, you were consider a minor until 21. Which meant she couldn't rent her own house.

If her mom wanted her home one call to the cops and it was a wrap. She would have no choice but to do as her mother say. The good news is her mother couldn't put her out since she was a minor.

It would be hell living there though. Looking up OB/GYN offices, Juniqua needed to make an appointment. She had missed enough days of school. Her plan was to attend school and find a part time job. None of her friends had talked to her since her pregnancy. For the first time, she was all alone.

Doing her hair she wanted to look nice her first day back at school. Getting up early, Juniqua went back into her old routine. Waking up her siblings, she made sure they got dressed and ate breakfast. The moment she stepped into the school. All eyes were on her, rumors were she got pregnant by one of the boys in a sextape.

She knew nothing about a sextape. That is until her friend Mark showed it to her on pornhub. The video had been put up by her ex, Tyjuan. It was old and had been up for a few months. If it wasn't one thing it was another.

That's probably why Elijah was treating her like shit. In the video Juniqua was at a party last year going down on Tyjuan and his friend. She had taken shots of vodka and popped a pill. Even in the video she looked gone and though she didn't remember being recorded. She remembered feeling sick and now she felt even sicker.

The stares she was getting made her feel like shit. She couldn't even concentrate on her schoolwork. Tyjuan didn't make it any easier either.

"Do sumn for the camera for the one time Juicy."

He yelled while she stood at her locker.

As if the timing couldn't be more right. The hallway was filled with people who heard it all. Leaving the school, Juniqua called Elijah's mom Joy.

Unable to talk she cried so hard.

"Slow down baby tell me what happened what's wrong?" Joy asked.

She tried to tell her the short version. Half an hour later Joy was pulling up. On the ride back to the house, Joy wanted to talk to her mother. Her mother wanted nothing to do with the situation.

Joy decided to just take the girl back to Canton. Taking her to pick up a few new clothes. They went to sign in at Canton High. Without Juniqua's mother, they wouldn't transfer her. Juniqua wanted to scream, no matter what, she had to depend on her mother.

Wishing she could get emancipated, she surely would if she could afford to do just that.

"Listen let's see if she will at least sign a temporary guardianship agreement."

Joy said.

"I already know she won't, she wants me to suffer. Thanks for everything you tried to do. I will figure it all out when the baby comes."

Juniqua said.

"I'm gonna look into getting you some help, alright? You shouldn't have to live like that."

Joy said.

"It's okay, I just have to stick it out. If Miss Jasmine gives me a ride I will work every day even on weekends. I might as well make as much money as I can. That way I can start buying the baby stuff."

Juniqua said.

"Don't worry about that right now. I will help you get things for the baby. Get through school and everything will work itself out."

Joy told her.

"Thanks for helping me. I know with me and Elijah's situation, you probably unsure about whether I'm telling the truth. I wouldn't lie to you about something as serious as a child."

Juniqua said.

"I believe you and I also understand we all have things we've done in our past. You can't apologize that it happened and you have to move on and grow from it. No judgment here, okay? Anytime you ever want to talk, don't hesitate to call me up no matter what time it is."

Joy smiled.

"I will, thanks again Miss Joy."

She said getting out of the car.

Juniqua walked into the house and saw that it was a mess. Her mother's boyfriend had left beer bottles and ashtrays filled with blunt roaches. All along the coffee table and living room floor.

"Oh, it's you, I thought you was ya momma."

Shawn said walking into the living room startling her.

"Where is my mom, I thought she was off work today?"

Juniqua asked.

"She ran yo auntie to the store a minute ago. What you doing home from school early for?"

He asked.

"I didn't feel well."

She replied walking past him to her room.

Shawn followed her down the hall and Juniqua's heart began to race. Running to her room she tried to shut her bedroom door. Shawn stopped it with his foot and shoved his weight up against the door. With him being stronger she stumbled backwards. Shawn pushed and held her down on the bed. Juniqua screamed and tried to fight him off of her.

"They say pregnant pussy is the best pussy, let's find out."

He said as he pulled his erection through his boxers opening.

Grabbing her by the back of her head, he punched her in the face repeatedly before forcing her on her stomach.

"Please don't!... Let me gooooooooooo... stooooooop it please!"

Juniqua cried out.

He pulled down her pants along with her panties. Juniqua tried to wiggle out from underneath his grip.

"Hold still lil bitch!"

He huffed placing his elbow in her back.

Pressing his weight down, Juniqua let out a low moan in excruciating pain. She couldn't breath and her eyes swelled up with tears. Feeling the head of his penis at her opening she anticipated more pain to come.

Closing her eyes, Juniqua wanted this all to be over. Why was all of this happening to her? Her unborn child would be exposed to all of this. Feeling faint, Juniqua gasped for air struggling to breathe. This is not how she planned on dying. Silently she prayed to God to spare her child.

Suddenly she felt all of his body weight collapse at once on top of her. Crawling her way from him, she looked up to see Joy standing there in tears with a frying pan in her hand. Rushing in her arms Juniqua was glad to see her face.

"Thank God you came inside he was trying..."

She sobbed unable to get the words out.

"I know, it's alright now, I'm going to call the police. You can't stay here sweetie it's not safe for you or the baby."

Joy said in tears.

She knew first-hand how it felt to be forced to have sex.

"What the fuck is going on in here?"

Juniqua's mother spat.

"What's going on is, he was trying to rape her and I plan on seeing that he gets arrested. Had I not came in to give her the phone she left in my car, no telling what all he would have done to her. Either you sign over guardianship or I will see to it that every news headliner, have that ugly mugshot of your punk ass boyfriend. What its gone be, because we can take the both of you to court. I guarantee after you pay court cost you won't have a pot to piss in nor a window to throw it out of. Fuck with me if you want to."

Joy spat.

"I'll sign whatever you need me to."

Her mother said.

"Then get to signing, I got the paper right here."

Joy said handing her the document.

"Don't it have to be notarized?"

Her mother asked.

"Just so happens I'm licensed to notarize."

Joy said with a smile.

Jasmine had bugged her to get licensed right after their father's funeral. Pulling out her notary stamp, Joy quickly stamped the document.

"This says four years, you ain't keeping her that long."

Her mother said in disbelief.

"She'll be legal in four years, so yes I will."

Joy replied.

"Well I don't know how she gone get her social and birth certificate. I don't have it and I sure as hell ain't getting it for her."

She spat.

"Then we can make you eligible for the show, inmate wives and turn his pedophile ass in."

Joy replied.

"Fine, but if she loses this copy she S.O.L."

Her mother said leaving the room to go get the documents Juniqua needed.

Joy waited until she returned with the papers. Tossing the papers at Juniqua, her mother showed no compassion.

"Let's go, don't even worry about it.'

Joy said trying to comfort her.

Handing Joy her birth certificate and social security card, They left and got inside the car. Juniqua didn't know what hurt worst. Almost being raped or having a mother that could care less. The entire ride back to Canton Juniqua cried. Joy allowed her that moment to release all the hurt. No child should go through what she was going through.

"Tomorrow we can start the process of having you transferred. Get you some clothes and get your schedule to work. Don't let what happened today hinder you from becoming the woman you were destined to be. Be better than the people that hurt you. Forgive them and fight through this and I plan on being there every step of the way. We can't give up, we can make each other strong. I won't give up on you if you don't give up on me. I'm new to this parenting stuff so I'm learning along the way."

Joy said.

'You already a better mother than mine. I just don't understand why she hates me so much."

Juniqua sniffled.

"It's more of her unhappy with herself. Once she realizes what she's missing out on she'll regret it."

Joy told her.

"Now all we gotta do is make sure that you and Elijah agree to keep your bodies apart."

Joy said with a raise of her brow. They both looked at one another and laughed.

"I am sorry about that but we are done as far as that. He's moved on and I'm more focused on my baby. You don't have to worry about that ever again."

Juniqua assured her.

"Good now let's get you on fleek for your first day at Canton high."

Joy smiled.

"Now Miss Joy what you know about on fleek?"

She laughed.

"You and my son going to stop sleeping on me I'm hip."

Joy said laughing.

"My bad, you hip."

Juniqua said with a smile.

Chapter Eight

Joy

"Wordplay"

"This is tough right here."

Charlene said concentrating on the words on the scrabble board.

"You can always skip and let me get my points."

Joy smiled.

"No way I got this just give me a sec."

Charlene said.

Deep in thought, Joy noticed how she bit down on her lip whenever she got frustrated.

"Would you like more wine?"

Joy asked.

"No thank you and my word is E.R.O.T.IC, erotic."

She said doing a victory dance.

"Now tell me exactly what do you know about erotic?"

Joy flirted.

"Erotically speaking a lot."

Charlene replied.

"I stand corrected, please proceed."

Joy said.

"Wouldn't you like that."

She laughed.

Joy and Charlene had been getting quite close. The day she spoke to Nathan, he decided to work things out with his ex-wife. Not that she had wanted more than friendship. She simply didn't want to fight anymore. They agreed to move past it and focus on other important things.

Right now Charlene was everything she wanted. Only something still was missing. They had moments whenever the sexual tensions would rise. However, whenever it past her thoughts would revert back to Nathan.

Charlene wanted to take things slow. While Nathan wanted to be exclusive immediately. If only Charlene was Nathan and he was her.

"It's getting late my kids are on their way home."
Charlene said.

"It's what nine o'clock can't we play a few more minutes?"
Joy asked.

"Joy I like you and all but I'm not ready for my kids to meet anyone new in my life yet."
She said.

"Not a problem I understand that. Just call me when you get a chance."
Joy told her before grabbing her keys and coat.

Joy used the bathroom before leaving. As she went to wash her hands she noticed aftershave on the sink. Opening the medicine cabinet there was men cologne, deodorant and shaving cream. Which explains why she always had a specific time to meet up.

Joy was the type to give everyone a fair shot. Without actual facts, it all meant nothing. On her way out a blue Pontiac Grand Prix pulled up. A stud hopped out of her car with kids in tow. Joy saw everything crystal clear now. It wasn't a man that lived there, it was a stud. The look Charlene gave was more so apologetic. Joy was done being a fool for both Charlene and Nathan.

"Well I guess I will see you some other time Charlene."
Joy said getting in her car.

"Who the hell is she?"
The stud said pointing at Joy.

"Nobody Lyn, can you please not do this tonight."
Charlene said.

"Oh so you going to lie to her about me?"
Joy said fed up with the games.

"Who the hell are you?"
The girl asked.

"Ask your girlfriend who I am."
Joy spat.

"Joy don't do this."
Charlene said.

"Joy? So you been seeing her while I'm at work?"
The stud yelled.

"Oh no she made it clear she wanted to take things slow right."

Joy said.

The stud walked into the house and Charlene followed behind her. After the door was shut Joy went back inside of her car.

Driving home, Joy saw a dark sedan driving up the street slowly.

"Wonder what are the undercover police doing in this neighborhood."

She said.

Elijah was getting out of Jackson's truck when she pulled into the driveway.

"Hey sis, yo boy passed his written test. So we had to celebrate and practice for the driving test. I think somebody's ready for their first car."

Jackson said.

"Way to get your uncle to lay it on thick. If you want a car Elijah, you better get a job. Bring that defense up and keep those grades up. Then I might consider getting you a car."

Joy said.

"It was worth a shot."

Jackson chuckled.

"Hey big brother, how you holding up?"

Joy asked hugging him.

"Carmen pretty much moved on, think it's time I do the same. I really wish you and Jas would come by the house. There's things in that house that I can't explain Joy."

Jackson said.

"You're beginning to sound like a broken record. Elijah get cleaned up and tell your aunt Jas, David called me again for her."

Joy said.

"She still avoiding him?"

Jackson asked having a seat on the porch swing.

"Look Jackson before we sold the house I seen momma standing looking out the window. She was smiling like she was at peace. We all see things we can't explain."

Joy said.

"I wished what I witnessed was that pleasant. Joy I remember being in the living room. Next thing I know it was like I was traveling through time. Daddy's childhood wasn't normal Joy. That don't excuse him for what he done. Just saying what was done to him wasn't right either. Our grandfather was evil J, so evil it fucked daddy up. Forced him to do what he thought he had to do. Which was kill the monster, that monster was our grandfather. Now I know I might seem crazy but listen to me. That house is filled with souls, unfreed souls and one of them being daddy's. You read the letters daddy was seeing momma's spirit. You forgave daddy and you said momma was at peace. I'm the only one that haven't forgiving him J. I want to but I also need to know what created all of this. Something unnatural killed that boy. The old lady seen it and I done seen it. This thing is growing and becoming stronger. We have to get rid of it and help free daddy's soul."

Jackson said.

"Do you hear yourself, seriously Jackson daddy is dead. Nothing is wrong in that house. As far as the guy that got killed who knows what happened. We wasn't there to witness the truth."

Joy said.

"Joy listen to me, there is something evil in that house. Now I plan on doing something about it. Whether you help me or not."

Jackson said

"I guess you don't need me after all."

Joy said.

"I have to get to work soon tell Jas I said hey."

He said before heading towards his car.

"Jackson! Be careful and I can check into the house. We are family and sticking together is what we do."

Joy called out to him.

Jackson smiled, all he needed was his sisters support. Joy went inside the house and saw that Juniqua and Jas were watching How To Get Away With Murder.

"Now how y'all gone watch without me, what I miss?"

Joy said sitting next to Juniqua. Who was eating popcorn, and filling her in on what happened. The three were so into the show. That when Elijah asked about some scissors. He was shushed by all three of them.

"Dang, it's just a show."

He said.

"Boy will you shut the hell up."

Jasmine said.

When the show ended they caught up on Jane the virgin.

"See Michael is too much for me right now."

Jasmine said.

"Raphael is the one she need to watch. He got no good ass Petra on the prowl. She and Michael should just go on bout they life."

Joy said.

"Michael is a good choice for her."

Juniqua replied.

"See you two are so wrong, he didn't even want her to have the baby."

Jasmine argued.

Joy got a text from Nathan telling her to come outside.

"Give me a second while I go see what's up with Nathan."

Joy said leaving out.

"Don't do nothing I wouldn't do."

Jasmine said giving her a goofy smile.

Nathan was sitting in his truck. Joy got in on the passenger side.

"How you been?"

He asked her.

"I been ok, what's up what made you hit me up?"

Joy said.

"I can't stop thinking about you. I know you think it's all game but I'm dead ass."

He said.

"I been thinking about you too."

Joy admitted.

"So what's keeping us from being together?"

He asked.

"Aside from years of friendship and the fact your my son's coach."

Joy replied.

"Ride with me?"

He said starting up his truck.

"You said talk, not that you was going to kidnap me."

Joy teased.

Riding around, Nathan took them to a spot they often went to when they were kids.

"Remember when we used to ride our bikes to this park. Think we shared our first kiss here. Until you played me for what's his face."

Nathan said.

"Wow you remember that, that was ages ago."

Joy laughed.

"You tend to remember things that mean something to you."

He said.

"Nathan what's the reason you brought me out here?"

Joy asked.

"I don't know how else to tell you that I'm still in love with you."

He replied.

Leaning forward, Joy kissed him. Unsure of how she felt, she needed to see if whatever this was could be real. Deciding to no longer fight it, Joy let go of all her fears and uncertainties. Climbing on top of him, Joy and Nathan explored one another's bodies.

Tasting each other's tongue, Joy craved more.

"Are you sure you wanna do this right here?"

He asked.

"Shut up and take off my clothes."

Joy said.

"You don't have to tell me twice."

Nathan replied easing off her shirt.

Thumbing her areoles, Nathan flicked his tongue across her nipples. Joy lifted up and eased out of her leggings. Nathan pulled down his sweats and his hard dick sprang up. Placing her arms around his shoulders. Joy tried to relax as she eased down on his dick. Both were unable to control their breath.

Giving breathless kisses, Nathan moaned enjoying the feel of being inside her warm wet tightness. Gripping her waist Nathan enjoyed the ride. Winding her hips, Joy did a rise and fall. When it got too good she bit down on her bottom lip. From slow and sensual to straight fucking.

Joy screamed out as he hit a spot that caused her knees to buckle. The truck bounced as Joy rode him like a bull master. Feeling the intense tingle from his toes up, Nathan gripped her shoulders as he climaxed.

"Oh my God is this what I been missing?"

Joy smiled.

"That and much more."

He smiled.

"As much as I enjoyed that, I still think we should be friends."

Joy said.

"Damn Joy, you sure can ruin a moment."

Nathan said.

"Excuse me for caring about our friendship."

She said.

"If you felt that way, why even take it there."

He spat.

"First off you need to watch your tone. Second I never changed up about the way I felt. Third take me the hell home."

Joy said.

"Look either we be friends or lovers because I'm done playing these games with you."

Nathan said.

"I guess you have your answer friend."

Joy replied.

"Why are you so afraid of being with me?"

He asked.

"Could we please just go already I'm done talking."

Joy said slipping back into her clothes.

Nathan did exactly what she wanted him to.

Parking out front of her house, Joy rushed out of his truck. Maybe she was overreacting a bit but still she didn't want to up and jump into something again like she always managed to do.

"So what happened with you?"

Jas asked.

"Remind me why I even waste my breath speaking to that asshole."

Joy spat.

"You two beefing again I swear y'all need Dr. Phil or Iyanla to fix y'all lives."

Jasmine said.

"What I need is new friends and to come home to a quiet house."

Joy said as she headed for the shower.

Jasmine would have flipped if she found out her and Nathan hooked up. So, for now she would keep it to herself. The rollercoaster relationship they had was beginning to stress her. Maybe it was for the best that they didn't take it further.

Checking her phone as if she was expecting him to call. Joy thought about how hurt he was about her decision. Had she messed up and he was done trying for good?

"You bugging, who cares if he wants to be done."

Joy said back to her reflection in the bathroom mirror.

Joy had passion marks along her collarbone. Running some bathwater, she placed bath beads in the water. Stepping into the water, Joy eased in. Enjoying the feel of the hot water against her skin, Joy's phone rung and she damn near broke her neck thinking it was Nathan.

Charlene was calling and Joy let it go to voicemail. The entire night she constantly checked her phone. Nodding on and off, Joy's eyelids were getting heavier.

"Joy, there is a girl and two kids at the door for you."

Jasmine said standing in her bedroom doorway.

Joy tossed the covers back and got up. She knew damn well Charlene hadn't stooped so low as to use her little girls. Walking into the living room, Joy hardly recognized Charlene. Her lip was busted, nose looked broken and her right jaw was puffed out like a blow fish.

The side of her face bruised and turning purple. Her left eye was completely shut and the right was as red as fire. Unable to speak out of her swollen lips. Charlene stood trembling, in an attempt to try and explain why she was at Joy's door at two in the morning.

"Jasmine can you take these princesses in my bathroom, get them cleaned up for me."

Joy said.

"Come on babies it's alright follow aunt Jasmine and let's get you all clean."

Jasmine smiled at the girls.

Joy helped Charlene into the guest bathroom. Juniqua woke up and saw Joy helping her into the bathroom.

"Oh my God is she okay?"

Juniqua asked.

"Juniqua turn on the bathroom light and wet me a face towel with warm water."

Joy said.

"Yes ma'am."

Juniqua replied rushing to do as she was told.

Putting the lid down on the toilet. Joy helped Charlene sit down so she could get cleaned up.

"Juniqua sweetie can you clean her up for me, put some ice on that afterwards for the swelling. Charlene don't worry I will take care of everything."

Joy said going to grab the first aid kit.

"Joy you might want to cone take a look at this."

Jasmine said with a worried look.

"Juniqua, here's everything you might need in the first aid kit. Thank you so much for helping sweetie."

Joy told her.

"No problem Miss Joy I got this."

She replied with a smile.

Joy followed Jasmine into her master bathroom.

The two little girls were in the tub. The youngest one was playing with bubbles. While the older girl was in tears at the other end of the tub. She couldn't have been no more than six.

"Joy this baby has been abused, look at this child's back."

Jasmine said in tears.

Joy got on her knees and tried to talk to the little girl.

"Hi sweetheart my name is Joy. May I ask what's your name?"

Joy asked.

"Tiffany"

The girl said above a whisper.

"That's a pretty name Tiffany. Sweetie are you in pain if you are can you tell me where?"

Joy asked.

"My...my back...and my bad touch part."

The little girl said in tears. She was so afraid she began to shake.

"I'm just going to take a look at your back honey."

Joy said as she helped the little girl lean forward.

Joy took a look at all the whelps on her back. Tears begin to fall freely, she had seen this before with her own brother. When their father often beat him with electrical cords and such. Her skin had split in some places while in other parts of her back was bruised and infected. Jasmine was so emotional she had to walk away.

"Jas, I need you sister help me get her out of the tub."

Joy called out to her.

Juniqua walked in after Jasmine and saw the little girls back. Covering her mouth Juniqua teared up as well.

"Hey listen this girl has been abused we must get her to the hospital. Did you get Charlene cleaned up for me?"

Joy asked her.

"Almost, I need more ointment. Who in the world could do such a thing?"

Juniqua asked.

"Her lover, but you bet your last dollar she won't get away with this."

Joy said.

"She? You mean a pathetic ass bi..."

Jasmine spat but was cut off when Joy made a face that said calm down.

"Joy we gotta do something."

Jasmine said.

"I'm down for whatever too."

Juniqua said.

"You both are pregnant, I can't risk either one of you getting hurt.'

Joy said.

"I'm licensed to carry, you ain't said nothing but a word."

Jasmine replied.

"Juniqua I need you to get the girls safe in my room. I have t-shirts they can wear. If you can get the oldest to tell you what happened and how long, we can report it to the cops. Take your time with her she's scared."

Joy told her.

Jasmine and Joy went to check on Charlene.

"I need for you to try and talk. You can start by telling me why Tiffany is scared to death. She has been beaten and molested. How could you let such a thing happen?"

Joy said filled with rage.

"Joy I ...didn't know...I was asleep…"

Charlene struggled to talk.

"You was sleep and then what?"

Jasmine asked.

"I... heard Tiffany crying. Lyn was n...not in bed so I went and checked. That's when I saw Lyn on top of my baby. Joy I fought for my babies and ran."

Charlene cried.

"How the hell can a woman rape a child."

Jasmine said confused and upset.

"I seen her she's a stud, the manly dominant females. She probably used a strap on dildo."

Joy said.

"Sick bitch."

Jasmine spat ready to go find that girl.

"Charlene where is Lyn at now?"

Joy asked.

"The h…house."

She replied weakly.

"We have to call the police, that girl is traumatized. Why would you even want that around them?"

Joy said still upset for her allowing it to happen.

"Joy I moved twice...she...she keeps finding us."

Charlene said.

"Well that's ok cause I got something for that bitch she won't be back."

Jasmine said.

"When I get back we are going to the hospital and the police. Jasmine let's go we can't let her get away."

Joy said.

"Momma who is that, what's going?"

Elijah asked.

"A friend, look call the police help Juniqua with Charlene and the girls. Lock the doors behind me and don't answer for nobody but the police. Call me if someone else comes over."

Joy said as she put on a sweatshirt, some sneakers and sweatpants. Jasmine followed suit and dressed comfortable in a pull over hoody and jogging pants.

"Close yo eyes sis."

Jasmine said as she applied Vaseline on Joy's face. Joy took the grease when her face and neck was greased up. Jasmine then closed her eyes as Joy applied some to her face and neck. The two sisters were ready for whatever as they got in Joy's car.

"Let's go I got my M.T.T so we good."

Jasmine said zipping up her purse.

"M.T.T what's that?"

Joy asked while pulling out the driveway. "Mace, taser and my twenty-two, I wish a bitch would!"

Jasmine said pumped.

"You been watching Love & Hip-Hop again?"

Joy asked laughing.

"Nope bad girls club."

Jasmine laughed.

Once they got to Charlene's house they heard loud bangs and glass shattering. "Oh this heffa done lost her mind." Jasmine said.

"Hand me the gun, if anyone going down its gone be me."

Joy said holding out her hand.

Jasmine gave her a we in this together look. Taking the pistol, Joy tucked it inside her pocket. The front door was open so Joy was the first to step inside the house.

The house was wrecked, furniture cut up, tables turned over. Now dishes were being thrown from the kitchen.

"Bitch think she can run from me! I own that bitch she belong to me!"

The voice yelled from in the kitchen.

"You don't own nobody!"

Joy said loud enough to get her attention.

"Who the fuck is that? Who up in my house?"

She yelled.

"Bring yo ugly ass up in here and find out."

Joy spat.

The girl stepped into the living room. Joy couldn't understand for the life of her, what Charlene see in her. The girl was funny looking. Real dark and favored rapper Hurricane Chris.

Look like she was about to up and say Aye bay bay. Her braids swayed and the beads on the ends clicked.

"Looking like something off orange is the new black."

Jasmine spat.

"The fuck you bitches doing in my house?"

The girl yelled.

"You mean Charlene's house, you fake ass wanna be man! It's bitches like you that make me sick. You don't do shit up in this bitch but scratch yo stanking ass! That girl don't want you and yo dusty bum ass keep stalking her. What, nobody else want yo cock roach looking ass?"

Joy spat.

"Bitch who you think you talking to?"

The girl yelled as she ran up.

Joy did a quick side step and Jasmine closed lined her. Placing her foot on her throat, Joy aimed the gun at her head.

"You miserable sick ass worthless bitch. How dare you put your nasty ass hands on a child. You deserve to rot in jail but first we gone do a little makeover on you."

Jasmine smiled.

Joy stepped back long enough to raise her other foot and bring it down stomping her face. They took turns whooping her ass.

"Get yo ass up!"

Joy spat pointing the gun to her. She made the girl walk outside to the car.

"Get in the motehrfuckin' trunk!"

Jasmine spat.

"Fuck both of you bitches."

The girl said.

Joy gave her a hard right hook to her face. Jasmine countered back with a quick left jab.

"Damn I forgot about my rings shit that hurt!"

Jas spat.

Joy pushed her in the trunk and drove back to her house. The police were already there when they arrived. Joy quickly parked and popped the trunk. Yanking the girl out, Joy shoved her up to the porch.

"Here's the perp thank us later."

Jasmine said to one of the officers.

"You ladies cannot take the law into your hands."

The officer said.

"We know, that's why we brought her back still breathing."

Joy said.

The officer gave a stern look before reading her rights.

"Next time, let us do our job please."

He said before hauling her away in the back of the cop car.

"Try to be a good citizen and this the thanks we get."

Jasmine said.

"Momma they took Charlene to the hospital in the ambulance."

Elijah told her.

"I'm going to head down there."

Joy said.

A social worker was asking the girls questions. Joy knew Charlene was a good mother but in this situation, it made her look bad. With the state stepping in there was no telling where those little girls would end up.

"The last thing them babies need is to be shuffled around in the system."

Jasmine said.

"Could be placed somewhere worse off. They don't see it like that though."

Joy said.

Heading over to the hospital, the girls were being checked out. Both Jasmine and Joy stayed there all night. Charlene's parents ended up coming to the hospital to get the girls. She was being placed into custody for questioning about the abuse. Joy hoped that she wasn't involved with those girls being abused. These days you couldn't put nothing pass anyone.

You definitely couldn't trust everyone with your kids. Which is exactly why Jasmine planned on raising her child herself. She would be damn if her child gets harmed by one of David's down low partners.

Joy thought about her unborn grandchild. She didn't want Elijah having random girls near her grandchild. Same thing goes for Juniqua. Tonight, was an eye opener and it broke their hearts that those poor girls had to go through that.

Chapter Nine

Jasmine

"Fantasy"

Walking into the house, Jasmine followed the trail of rose petals. The sounds of Jodeci's "Freak You" playing in the background. Candles were lit throughout the house. Jasmine's heels clicked with every step she took.

Standing in the living room by the all-white grand piano. Jalen smiled back at her, he had pulled out all the stops. Looking nothing but the best. He wore white slacks and an all-white open button up.

His chiseled pecks and perfect six pack of abs displayed. Motioning with his finger he gestured for her to come closer. Jasmine sashayed to him and greeted him with a kiss.

"It's about time I show you just what you been missing."

He said placing her on top of the piano.

A bowl of fresh strawberries and a can of Redi whip was on the side of her. Jalen began ripping off her dress. Hungrily he eyed her body and planted kisses along her neck. Grabbing a strawberry, he fed her one. Shaking the can of whip cream, with a devishly smirk.

Jasmine pulled him close inviting her tongue inside his mouth. Laying her back Jalen removed her panties. He had her right where he wanted her. Jasmine didn't object to anything he was about to do. As he proceeded to spread her thighs, Jalen ran his fingers between her pussy lips. Gasping from pleasure Jasmine was in heaven.

"Ooooh baby that feels so good."

She moaned.

"I figured you would enjoy that. Jasmine baby I need to feel inside of you. Let me make you feel better, I promise you won't regret it."

Jalen said.

"Yes baby I need you too."

Jasmine moaned. Jalen picked her up and sat down on the piano bench. Easing Jasmine down on top of his erection. He filled her up as they began to make their own music. Jasmine rode him as her fingers slid along the piano keys.

"Tell me you love it baby!"

Jalen said as he stroked her harder and faster.

"I..I.. ahhhhh... I love....it!"

She screamed out.

"That's right baby, say my name Jasmine."

He demanded.

"Jalen…mmmm...Jalen…ahhhhh…Jalen....ohhhhhh Jalen its coming!"

Jasmine moaned as she felt the waves of an orgasmic all time high. Her juices trickled down her thighs. Jalen held her close as he moaned and kept stroking her.

"Jasmine!"

David yelled busting in the house aiming gun.

"David, no wait I can explain!"

Jasmine said as she began to panick.

"Jasmine...Jasmine"

David yelled over and over with tears in his eyes.

He charged towards them both and the gun went off. ***Boom!*** Gasping Jasmine sat up, looking around she was in bed.

"Jasmine what the hell is wrong with you?"

Joy said turning on the lamp.

"It seemed so real."

Jasmine said.

"Damn it Jas, you knocked over my clock."

Joy said when she noticed it wasn't on the other nightstand.

"Joy like I almost died David walked in on me and Jalen. I mean it was getting good too. He set the mood, had the strawberries and Jodeci. He had me hitting notes like Whitney back in 87'. Then here come David's confused ass fucking up our moment."

Jas went on and on.

"Whose Jalen?"

Joy asked with a motherly tone.

"J, don't even give me that look, the point is David might do something stupid."

Jasmine changed the subject.

"Who is this Jalen guy? Obviously, you having fantasies about him. With yo strawberries and Jodeci. We all know when Jodeci and strawberries gets involved it ends in getting pregnant. Did you have an affair before all that stuff went down with David?"

Joy asked.

"No Joy damn, Jalen is a friend of mines brother. Who happens to live next door because his mother is ill. We saw each other the other day. Started catching up, had lunch and kissed. I went home, he went his way and I kept my distance. Nothing else to talk about we just cool that's it."

Jasmine said all in one breath.

"Back up to the part where you kissed the next-door neighbor. Who also just happens to be your friend's brother. Jas that's like two violations right there. Not to mention that yo ass still very much married."

Joy said.

"I know Joy, you don't have to remind me of what I already know. It wasn't like I planned on him kissing me. We know it was wrong that's why I didn't tell yo ass."

Jasmine spat.

"Well its much bigger, now that you dreaming about fucking my neighbor!"

Joy replied.

"I don't need this shit I can go home."

Jasmine said.

"So you plan on working things out with David?"

Joy asked.

"Shit, I don't know what I'm going to do."

Jasmine said.

"Sooner or later you're going to have to face him."

Joy said.

"I know and I will sis, I didn't mean to snap at you. The whole kiss thing threw me off."

Jas said.

"It's cool, but whoever this Jalen guy is try to keep your lips off of him. At least until you divorce David or figure out what it is you going to do."

Joy said.

"That's easier said than done, he is too damn fine!" Jas said.

"I said try damn it or do I need to pay Jalen a visit. You know I will."

Jasmine said rolling her eyes.

"Whatever and if you had a wet dream go wash yo ass. Matter of fact just move I'm changing the sheets."

Joy said getting out of bed.

"We are sisters so keep it real. Don't act like you don't have those dreams either."

Jasmine said helping her strip the bed.

"Jas, you too close back up now."

Joy said trying to get past her.

"Just like when we were kids always running from germs."

Jasmine teased.

"For real Jasmine if you don't keep them coochie dipped fingers of yours away from me. Stop playing now for real move!"

Joy said while backing up.

"Coochie dipped I got yo dipped."

Jasmine said laughing.

She chased Joy around the house. It felt like old times without all the pain Joy endured.

"It's good having you home sis."

Jasmine smiled.

"Glad to be back."

Joy said.

Jasmine decided it was time to get her shop back in order. Tired of moping around she knew work would take her mind off of it. After her morning coffee, Jas headed for the door to start her day.

Not paying attention, she was too busy checking her emails on her phone. That she didn't notice Jalen working on his mother's yard. Cutting off the lawn mower, he walked over to her.

"Good morning stranger."

He said.

"Good mor…oh sweet baby Jesus!"

Jasmine said as she looked up to see a shirtless Jalen.

"Did I scare you?"

He said confused.

"Kind of, listen I really would appreciate if we were not to do this."

Jasmine said.

"As you wish you enjoy your day."

Jalen said before walking away. Jasmine got in her car and drove to her shop. She felt bad about pushing Jalen away like that. So bad that she decided to call David up.

"Hello?"

He answered on the first ring.

"David, we need to discuss some things are you busy around noon?"

She asked.

"No, want me to come to your sister's house to talk?"

He said.

"No we can meet at the diner near my dad's house."

She replied.

"Okay see you then."

He hung up.

Something didn't feel right, Jasmine knew her dream was not too farfetched. Business was a slow pace and noon was approaching. David was already at the diner when she arrived. He looked a mess too. The thick five o'clock shadow and bags under his eyes showed the stress.

"Hey you look nice."

He stood as she walked up to the booth.

Sliding in across from him she was at a loss for words. The David she knew was handsome, honest and ambitious.

"You don't look too well, is everything alright?"

Jasmine asked concerned.

"I'm fine, taking some time off from the force. Work on us for a while, you are wanting to work things out right?"

He asked.

"Actually, I wanted to talk about us ending on a good note. I thought about it and I just can't get past the idea of you being with another man. You need to figure out what drove you to do that."

Jasmine said.

"Damn it Jasmine, I already told you it was a mistake."
David said hitting the table causing her to jump.
Other people begin to look at them.
"David look at you, something is serious wrong with you.
Go get help and if you need me as a friend I will be there."
She told him.
"Is there someone else Jasmine? Who is he? Tell me because
I promise you that I intend on taking care of'em personally."
David said with a faraway look.
"Excuse me, I don't take kindly of threats. Now I am saying
this as nicely as I can. We are over, I want a divorce. Either you
sign the papers willingly or we can do this the hard way. You
messed up, not me, you cheated on me. It wasn't the other way
around so deal with it."
She said.
"This isn't over Jasmine, not until I say it is."
David said.
"Get help David."
Jasmine said before leaving.

Heading down to the police station, Jasmine filed a
restraining order against David. He seemed off and she wanted
to be safe. Giving her lawyer the greenlight to serve papers for a
divorce. She felt relieved to be getting it over and done. Around
three, Juniqua came into the shop for her first day.
Joy decided to help out on delivery orders. The three of them
decided to close shop at six.
"Hey is that car always across the street like that."
Joy said noticing it was an unmarked police car.
"Shit that might be David, he didn't take it well when I
asked for a divorced. I already placed a restraining order against
his ass."
Jasmine said.
"You shouldn't have to go through all of that."
Joy said.
"You would think so, but I don't put anything past anybody
anymore."
She said.
They left and the unmarked car pulled up right after that.

"I knew that this shit was going to happen."

Jasmine mumbled.

Calling her lawyer, she made sure to tell her everything. If this was going to be a war she planned on giving him one hell of a fight. Not even telling him about her pregnancy. Jasmine wanted to keep it to herself until she made her moves.

"You might have to speed up the process if he's starting to stalk you."

Joy told her.

"Now you believe me when I say he's not all the way there. He looked so crazy when we met at the café."

Jasmine said.

"I'm also getting licensed to carry and that's all to it."

Joy said serious.

"Fine with me, I just want to get this divorce over with."

She said.

"Speaking of over with, who is that with Nathan?"

Jasmine pointed out across the street at the bakery shop.

"Oh, that would be his ex-wife, apparently, they working things out."

Joy said.

"Damn sis, well I am sure another man will come around."

Jasmine told her.

"Or woman and I told you me and Charlene are taking things slow."

Joy smiled.

"I wish you get over all these high school crushes."

Jasmine teased.

"You just end the relationships before jumping in new ones with neighbors."

Joy joked.

"That's low even for you but I guess you get that one off."

Jasmine said.

"You knew better coming for me. Let's eat out, I don't feel like cooking."

Joy said.

"That's fine, Juniqua sweetie you did good today."

Jasmine told her.

They all headed to grab food from the chicken shack. Jasmine paid attention to the parked car in her review mirror as she pulled off. The car pulled into traffic two cars behind her.

This couldn't have been a coincidence. David was really taking things too far. Shaken up, Jasmine didn't know who she could go to for help. Deciding to keep quiet for the moment she kept it moving.

David was slumped over in the car as he tailed Jasmine. Hearing the words divorce caused his stomach to turn. Unable to concentrate on work, he was suspended until further notice. Even his parents questioned about his failed marriage.

Nobody knew the full story and he didn't want anyone to know. He made one mistake and was paying the ultimate price. Getting caught by a red light, David cursed and hit his steering wheel repeatedly.

Pulling out a pack of Newports from his shirt pocket. He placed a cigarette between his lips. The car lighter heated up as the light changed. Puffing away as he lit the cigarette he sped in search of Jasmine.

He had become obsessed with watching her. She looked so damn beautiful. He was reminded daily just how much of a fool he was, for allowing her to slip away. Unable to find her, he drove back home to the house they once shared. Boxes were still scattered throughout the house.

David hadn't moved anything. Instead he sat in a chair hoping for her to return. Calling her number over and over and unable to get an answer. David felt he was going insane without her. Nothing helped, not drinking, not crying or praying.

He was broken far more than he cared to be. Flashes of their honeymoon David missed her touch, her kiss even her smell he wanted it all back. Walking into the bedroom, David smelled her different fragrances.

The bed was unmade still and David hadn't slept in days. Going in his wife's panty drawer he sniffed all of her under garments. David undressed and put on her brassiere and panties. Laying in bed he massaged the material. Imagining that Jasmine was in his arms.

Touching himself, he moaned out her name. He would do anything just to have her back in his arms. After a quick climax, the loneliness feeling was back. Tossing and turning, he was unable to sleep.

What he was going through had him ready to end it all. The thought of seeing Jasmine with someone else angered him.

"No, no, no, nooo!"

He yelled as images filled his head.

Getting up, he changed clothes and jumped into his ride. Driving to Joy's house at three in the morning. He parked up the street and looked through a pair of binoculars. Around five Joy and her son were coming out of the house. David quickly started up his car and backed up.

He didn't want to be seen. The last thing he needed was to be charged as a stalker. He knew Jasmine was probably still asleep. He wanted nothing more than to see her. Parking a street over he ran in between houses. Once he was in Joy's backyard he tried checking for an open window.

"Hey what you doing back there!"

A neighbor yelled startling David.

He took off running towards his car. His heart raced at almost being caught and knew he was losing it.

"What am I doing?"

He cried as he laid his head on his steering wheel. David heard sirens and knew it was best he get out of the neighborhood. The nearest place he could stay was Days Inn. Laying low for a while wouldn't be a bad idea.

Pulling out his phone he tried hacking her email and social media accounts. David was able to get through on her Facebook. Searching her messages back from when they first started talking. There were tons of messages from guys.

Her profile pic had changed and her relationship status read divorced. David's blood begin to boil, he was so mad. Finding a good pic of them together on his phone, he switched the profile pic and changed the status to married.

If she wanted a divorce she was not about to have it easy. David's plan was to wear her down. The way he did when he constantly asked her out. Before he made detective, David was a police officer. He met Jasmine her sophomore year of college.

She was visiting home from college. Her and a few friends had a wild party. Which resulted into the cops being called. The first thing Jasmine thought was that he was a stripper. She had felt him up and went to grab his gun. Until she seen there was an actual cop car parked out front.

"Oh my God I'm so sorry."

She said realizing he was a real cop.

"No need to, just try to keep it down."

He said tipping his hat.

Running into her for a second time. It felt as if it was fate as they eyed each other. This time they were in the grocery store. After he asked her out the rest was like a fairytale. A beautiful three years later and a ceremony. David never imagined it would all end like this.

He was logged out her account two hours later. She changed her email and password as well making it harder to hack. David began to pace not sure if Jasmine knew it was him. When his phone rung, it was her calling.

"Hello" he answered.

"David, why are you in my accounts? That's it, you have taken things too far. On top of that you want to peep through windows. It's over we can't be friends, I want nothing to do with you. I have a restraining order too! So next time you bring your ass over here you'll be locked up."

Jasmine spat.

"I didn't mean to upset anyone I just want to talk to you."

He said but was greeted with the dial tone.

Trying to call her back he got no answer. She must have placed him back on the block list. Maybe he did take things too far. All he wanted was to show her how much he missed her. Now she was going through all of this to keep him out of her life.

If he couldn't have her, then neither would anyone else. David loved her so much he'd kill her, before letting her be with another man.

Leaving the motel, he went out to get himself an untraceable gun. Soon as he got inside of the car he couldn't resist going to see Jasmine. Placing the gun purchase on hold. Instead, David was riding along the street that she lived on.

He parked and waited as everyone left one by one. Jasmine's car was still in the driveway. David sipped from a bottle of cognac. The neighbor guy made his way over. He watched as Jasmine smiled and greeted him at the door.

David felt numb he knew there had to be someone else. Stumbling out of his car he watched as Jasmine and the guy laughed and talked on the porch. David began to make his way across the street. Bottle in one hand and service pistol in the other.

His heart was beating out of his chest. The woman he loved was smiling and laughing for another man. David felt disrespected and he'd be damn if he continued to allow this to go on. Walking up the driveway Jasmine froze as she seen a disheveled David.

His eyes were glossed over and red from lack of sleep and being drunk. He swayed with every step he took. The look of hurt and humiliation painted across his face.

"David what are you doing here? I have a restraining order." Jasmine said backing up in the house.

"Jasmine go inside and lock the door call the cops." Jalen demanded.

David took another sip from his bottle and smiled.

"So I guess you are the man that's fucking my wife, huh?" David asked with a smile.

"No, look brother you had way too much to drink. Why don't you go sleep it off. The last thing you wanna do is do something stupid and end up sitting behind bars." Jalen said.

"I ain't your brother and how can fighting for the woman I love be stupid." David spat.

"It's not but she doesn't want you like this. Look at yourself man you think she married the guy I'm seeing now. Go sleep it off and fight for her the right way through your heart." Jalen told him.

"I already tried, I try and I try and she just keeps on breaking my heart." David cried.

"It takes time with women, now I'm not saying you do or don't have a chance. All I'm saying is give her a little more time."

Jalen said.

"I have given her plenty of time. I think now it's time for all of us to die!"

David said raising his gun up and pointing it at Jalen.

"Listen killing me won't solve a thing. In fact it's only going to make things worse."

Jalen said trying to keep him talkative until the cops showed.

A neighbor from across the street was on her phone. She mouthed the words are you okay. Jalen winked trying to not let David notice.

"What you winking for you gay or something?"

David asked cocking the gun.

Jalen placed his hands up as if he was being arrested.

"No, not gay there was something in my eye that's it."

He replied as a patrol car rode up.

"Sir I'm gone need for you to drop the gun and back up slow.""

The officer said.

Jalen eased down on his knees with his hands still in the air. David spun around and shot the officer twice.

"Now that there's no more distractions. Let's finish what we started Jasmine baby you might wanna bring your pretty little ass on up out of the house!"

David yelled.

"She's scared David look let's you and me work through this."

Jalen said.

"We don't have shit to work through."

David yelled.

"David stop please!"

Jasmine said peeping out of the front door.

"I will if you just come on out and talk to me." He said.

Jasmine took a deep breath she had already told the police, the officer they sent was down. She knew backup was on its way soon. Easing on the porch she carefully eased her way closer to the steps.

"You look so beautiful baby."

He said looking at her.

"David you have to stop this you're scaring me. You are upsetting the baby."

Jasmine held her stomach.

David's eyes lit up like a kid on Christmas.

"I'm going to be a father?"

He asked.

"Yes, but David you have to think about our child. Put the gun down please no one else has to get hurt."

Jasmine said.

"We can be together again just you, me and the baby."

David said.

"Yes we can go, so just put the gun down and let's go."

Jasmine said.

"I have to take care of the witnesses first baby."

David aimed the gun at Jalen.

"No David please don't, let's leave, look we can go anywhere."

Jasmine pleaded.

"I don't want to get caught so he has to be taking care of. Now either you get in the car or I kill you both."

David said.

Jasmine looked at Jalen and back to David.

"What you looking at him for did you fuck him?"

David aimed the gun at her.

"Oh God no! I didn't do that David I swear."

Jasmine was so scared she trembled.

"I'm not gone tell you again Jasmine."

David said with a far off look.

Jalen stood up and David turned and pulled the trigger. Jasmine screamed as Jalen collapsed holding his side which was bleeding out. Three police cars surrounded the house. All armed and aimed at David.

"Put the gun down boy!"

The sheriff said.

David grabbed Jasmine and pressed the gun to her head.

"You all got five minutes to leave or I'm killing us both."
David yelled.

"What's going on that's my sister!"
Joy said walking up.

The rode was blocked offed, news reporters were pulling up.
Ambulance sirens were going off and the entire block was
outside.

"Ma'am backup, this is a hostile situation."
A officer said. Joy saw David holding Jasmine with a gun
pressed up against her head.

"Oh my God, no please help my sister."
Joy cried.

"We will ma'am but you have to back up and let us do our
job."
The officer said.

Jackson, Mississippi officers along with special agents task
force were pulling up. David's former Chief came out to speak
with him. Joy called her brother to let him know what was going
on.

"David, son you don't want to do that let the girl go and just
take me."
The chief said walking up slowly.

"I don't want you chief all I want is my family. Now call off
the force and just let us go."
David said.

"I can't do that David and you know that."
The chief said.

David looked out at all the officers and knew he would rot in
jail a long time.

"I never meant for anyone to get hurt. I just wanted my
family chief."
David cried.

"I know so but you have to put the gun down and end this
madness now. I got an officer down and one man bleeding out.
They need to be hospitalized and if anyone of them die you will
be in much more trouble. I don't want that for you so let's save
these innocent lives."
The chief said.

The paramedics were behind the officers. The chief signaled for them to help the men that were down. Placing both men on stretchers they rushed them off. Chief continued to talk to David and Jasmine.

"I'm sorry baby."

David said turning Jasmine around to face him.

Putting the gun to his head he pulled the trigger. Blood splattered all over Jasmine as his body dropped. Unable to hear, Jasmine was being lifted off the ground.

The chief carried her towards the other officers. Jasmine could hear ringing and saw her mother's face before everything went black. Joy rushed to the ambulance as they placed Jasmine inside.

This was a shock to the entire town. David's lifeless body laying in front of her home. It was all too much for her to take in. She thanked God that he spared her sisters life.

At the hospital, Jasmine was still out of it and ended up having a miscarriage. Joy knew her sister would be devastated. Not knowing how to tell someone that their child didn't make it. After experiencing your husband commit suicide in front of you. Jasmine would have a nervous breakdown.

"I hope I'm not intruding, I had to make sure she was okay I'm Jalen."

The man introduced himself to Joy.

"Hi I'm her big sister Joy, she's sleeping for the most part. The baby didn't survive with the stress and high blood pressure. She doesn't even know about it yet."

Joy said sadly.

"Damn, you mind if I sit with her?"

Jalen asked.

"What are your intentions with my sister?" Joy asked.

"I care about her, we are just friends it's what she wanted. I'm not about to leave her side regardless of how I feel." He said.

"In that case you can stay, call me if she wakes up. I have to check up on my son."

Joy stood to leave.

Jalen eased in the chair, he was still in pain from his gunshot wound. Holding her hand, Jalen shedded a few tears. He worried the entire ride to the hospital. Unsure if he would see her again or not.

"Almost thought I lost you for a sec. Just to think I took a bullet today just because I couldn't stay away. I'd take another one again too if it meant I get to see your face again."

Jalen said.

"You are...so...damn...corny." Jasmine said smiling.

"You're awake, your sister just left I'll call her and let her know that you're up."

Jalen sat up.

"No just sing to me I could use a good song."

Jasmine said.

Jalen held her hand and sang the words to Raheem Davaughn's You. Drifting off as his sultry voice sent her peace. A single tear slid down her cheek as the cutest baby she had ever seen cooed in her mother's arms.

Jasmine had heard every word her sister and doctor said. She just wanted to grieve in peace. Her mother returned to show her that her child was in good hands. She could rest assure and no longer worry.

Jalen stopped singing when he heard her light snores. He was tired himself and decided to get some rest too. When Jasmine awoke from what she thought was a nightmare. She realized it wasn't just a dream. Jalen was beside her asleep in a chair. He was snoring so loudly she was amazed she slept through his snores.

"Welcome back sleeping beauty."

A nurse said walking in with a tray of food.

"I tried waking you both. You two were knocked out, how long have you both been married?"

The nurse asked.

"We're not, just friends."

Jasmine said as she sat up.

"This is some friend, he limped all the way from the ER to get to you. Make sure he doesn't put too much pressure on his wound. I brought up his prescription."

She said placing it on the stand.

"Jalen, Jalen wake up."

Jasmine tried to wake him up.

"You alright?"

He asked as he sat up.

"I will be now that you stopped snoring, sounded like a truck." Jasmine teased.

"Oh you got jokes ha, ha" he said wiping his eyes.

Jasmine saw him frown when he tried to get up.

"Jalen you're in pain, go get some rest."

Jasmine told him.

"I'm okay ain't no sense in leaving if you are about to be discharged too."

He said.

"I don't know if I'm going home or not." She said.

"Glad to have you back Miss Jasmine. How are you feeling?"

The doctor asked walking in.

"I feel fine its him I'm worried about."

Jasmine said giving Jalen the evil eye.

"Well let's check your vitals then we will take a look at your friend, sound good?"

The doctor asked.

"Yes. That's fine."

Jasmine said.

The doctor checked her blood pressure and gave her heart a listen.

"Looks good so you can go home Jasmine. Come back if the bleeding doesn't stop. We have brochures here for dealing with the loss of child. I strongly suggest you take it easy for at least a week."

The doctor said.

"Oh she will she has no choice."

Jalen said.

"As for you sir looks like you're straining that wound. Let's change that bandage and have a look."

The doctor said raising his shirt.

Jalen was bleeding through his bandage. The nurse came in and grabbed a few things to clean the wound. The doctor showed Jasmine how to clean it and to have him rest up for two weeks.

"Well that should about do it Mr. Smith you come back if it bleeds nonstop, okay?"

The doctor said before leaving.

They both were discharged and had no way home.

"I forgot we both got here in the ambulance. Let me call my sister and tell her we need a ride."

Jasmine said.

"I can cab it home no trouble at all."

Jalen said.

"No, we live right next door, it's not a problem."

Jasmine told him.

"Is this a bad time to tell you that even with a hospital bracelet on you look amazing."

He smiled.

"You are so corny."

Jasmine laughed.

"I just wanted to make you laugh."

He said.

"Thanks for being a good friend."

She told him.

Chapter Ten

Jackson

"My Father's Sins"

Jackson sat sitting on the living room floor. The therapist suggested that he try reaching out to his father. With candles lit and all of the lights out. He tried to reach the spirit of his father.

"Dad if you're here give me a sign."

Jackson said as he looked around.

The nearby bedroom door slowly creaked open.

"Dad is that you?"

Jackson asked looking down the hall.

A black figure ran past him and something crashed in the kitchen.

"He belongs to me!"

A voice said.

"No he doesn't why don't you face me!"

Jackson yelled standing up.

Whispers of voices surrounded him. Unable to understand their words because they all spoke at once. The room begin to spin and the candles flickered. A loud bang caused Jackson to jump.

The candles blew out and Jackson was pulled down to the ground. Hitting the back of his head he passed out. Moments later he stood looking down at his body laying there.

A young boy stood in the hall holding a lantern lamp. Jackson followed him and asked the boy who was he. The little boy placed a finger to his lips.

"Don't make too much noise he will find us."

The little boy said.

"Who will?"

Jackson whispered to the boy.

"The monster, my name is Jack...Jack Johnson."

He smiled.

Jackson's eyes widened, the boy was the young version of his father. The loud bangs where coming closer and young Jack grabbed Jackson's hand. They hid in a room in the closet.

Whatever this monster was it caused the entire house to shake. Jackson peeked out of the key hole. The bedroom door was kicked open. Jack turned off the lantern lamp so they wouldn't be caught.

Jackson seen the monster and his fiery eyes. This wasn't a ghost, that thing was something evil. *"A demon,"* Jackson thought to himself. The monster left and the loud bangs got fainter. Jack turned on the lantern and held Jackson hands.

"I can show you more just give me your hands."

The boy said.

Jackson held his hands and closed his eyes. When he opened his eyes, Jackson was inside of the house where he saw the old man with red eyes. The house looked different and a little girl was running outside. Jackson followed her and he saw the man in the rocking chair only he was younger. Stepping off the porch, Jackson saw the little girl playing with another girl.

"Stella don't go too far. stay in my sight you too Lorraine!"

The man yelled from the porch.

"Aunt Stella."

Jackson said shocked to see her so young.

Looking up, Jackson saw his father as a boy playing softball on the side of the house. The man on the porch yelled at young Jack.

"What I tell you about playing near my house boy!"

He said.

Young Jack looked afraid and tried to apologize. The man grabbed Jack by his ear. Pulling him into the house, Jackson ran to follow them. The man slapped the boy nearly knocking him down.

"Gone head on and get in that there back room."

He told him.

Jack began to cry as he walked into the room. Jackson followed them, it was like he was invisible anyway. Jack was forced to strip down and was beaten with a whip.

"Should of had your whore of a mother killed! Look at me boy look up at me like a man. As long as you are breathing I will treat you like the bastard child you are. You not my blood no how! Don't call me paw to you I'm Mister Johnson you got that!"

He yelled.

The boy nodded and he walked out of the room. It broke Jackson's heart to watch his father cry alone in his room. The room began to fade and Jack was much older. He was now around twelve or thirteen years old.

"Jack get yo simple minded ass out here boy!"

The man called out to him.

Jackson watched as Jack put his hat and coat on and took off to see what the man wanted. Following him the house looked changed around. Aunt Stella was in the kitchen she was a teen now.

"Stella don't burn the cornbread putting too much wood in that there stove!"

The man yelled.

"Yes paw I won't!"

She replied.

"Walter get out of momma cobbler and wait till dinner like everyone else. Or I'm gone tell paw what you doing."

Lorraine spat as she was icing a cake. Jackson walked out of the kitchen and outside where Jack was. He was chopping the head off a chicken.

"Gotdamn it Jack ring the chicken neck or I'm gone ring yours boy!"

The man yelled.

Jack tried ringing the chicken's neck and it hopped out his arms. The chicken ran and dragged its broken neck that dangled behind him.

"Catch him boy!"

The man yelled ready to hit Jack.

"Yes sir I'll get him."

Jack replied chasing the chicken.

After finally catching him, Jack placed the chicken's face down on the tree stump. Struggling to grab the ax and hold the chicken still.

"Give me the damn ax you just keep that bird real still."

Jack did as told and kept it steady. With one swift move the chicken's head fell to the ground. The feet still kicked and it scared Jack.

"He good as dead with no head. That there is just nerves making him move. It will pass in a few no need to think no different."

He said.

Jack nodded and proceeded to pluck the chicken. From what Jackson was seeing, now they were getting along. That is until everything faded again. Jackson was on a long gravel road. The sun was beginning to set and up ahead he saw a young Jack running.

Jackson heard screams coming from the opposite direction, Jack ran in. Walking towards the screams Jackson saw a young Lorraine being surrounded by white men. They kept raising her dress and pushing her around. One of them hit her in the head with a rock.

Knocking her out cold Jackson tried to fight the men off her. His hits didn't affect them one bit. He watched as his father's sister was being raped by white men. When each finished, they rode away leaving her laying there like a piece of trash. Jackson was so furious he wished he could kill each man.

"It's okay Jackson I'm free now."

Lorraine said standing behind him dressed in all white.

Jackson looked back and forth from Lorraine on the ground to the Lorraine standing beside him.

"Aunt Lorraine you died didn't you?"

Jackson asked.

"Yes, but it wasn't my brothers fault. Take me to him, where is he?"

She asked.

"I seen him running towards that way."

Jackson pointed.

"Take me to him please," she said smiling.

Jackson led the way towards were he saw his father running towards. They ended up back at the house. The old man was in his rocking chair. Jack ran up to him out of breath and trembling in fear.

"Paw...I...mean Mister Johnson its Lorraine. A bunch of white men surrounded her. It's was four of'em, one name was Tinsley."

Jack told.

"Tinsley boys got my little girl, you run next door tell Bobby to get his gun."

He said running in the house.

Jack quickly went and got the neighbor. A few pick-up trucks drove up in front of the house. Each armed and ready to defend in the name of one another. Both Jackson and Lorraine watched as the men sped off to fight in her honor.

"Daddy's too late and It wasn't Jack's fault." Lorraine said.

Jackson led Lorraine inside the house and into Jack and Walter's room. Lorraine watched him weep and sat beside him. She pointed to a blue bird in the window. Jack looked up and saw the bird, it was supposed to be a sign.

It was both Lorraine and Jack's favorite bird. Only seeing the bird made Jack even more saddened.

"I tried showing him a sign but he just didn't get it. Take me to the soul of Jack this is the past spirit."

Lorraine said.

Jackson was confused and then he remembered Jack and him was in a closet and he was merely showing Jackson the past.

"We can go to him after I see exactly what he wants me to see." Jackson replied.

"Okay Jackson." She smiled.

The front door slammed and the sound of furniture being tossed caused them all to jump.

"Daddy is upset with Jack. He is angry about my departure." Lorraine said sadden.

Jack stood up when the bedroom door opened.

"How many of them Tinsley boys was it?"

He asked.

"F... five Lorraine told me t...to run and get help. I came running straight to you Mister." Jack cried.

"You let them men kill and have they way with my little girl! It shoulda been you dead out there not my baby Lorraine."

He cried.

"I ran as fast as I could she… She told me to go get help." Jack wept.

Lorraine looked away as if she knew what was to come next. Jack was knocked down and strangled.

"You let them kill my baby and all you can say is you ran! Boy you will pay for this I promise you I will never forget this day! Dead or alive I will see to it that your bastard children pay for my Lorraine's death. You will hurt exactly how I hurt. To have your little girl violated and beaten! You hear me boy I swear for God I will make sure you reap this day."

He said menacingly.

Jack's mother came into the room and tried pulling him off of Jack. She was slapped and laid on the floor holding her face. Jackson knew the truth now, the whole truth. He was blamed for his sister's rape and murder. The house began to shake just like it had when the monster came.

"Hurry!"

A little boy's voice said.

"That's Jack, we have to go now!"

Lorraine said.

Jackson grabbed his aunt's hand and followed the voice. Walking into a dark path the two saw a lantern light in the far distance.

"Hurry the light is dimming."

Lorraine pointed.

Jackson refused to leave her behind, he carried her and ran towards the light. Both Jackson and Lorraine appeared in a closet with Jack.

"He's back, I have to turn off the light."

Jack said whispering.

The bedroom door creaked open. You could hear a hissing sound. The walls shook with its every step. Jackson looked through the key hole. The monster was reaching for the closet doorknob, until a faint knocking from afar could be heard. The monster quickly followed the sound in which it came from.

"Jack I finally found you!"

Lorraine hugged him.

"I'm sorry for not saving you."

Jack said hugging her back.

"It's not your fault Jack, daddy has turned evil. The day you killed him he turned to the dark world. I watched him Jack He's not my father anymore. I watched him takeover your body for years. He is the reason you did all of those bad things. Everyone is waiting for you Jack. Mom, Pauline, grandma and grandpa. I came back for you brother. Your son is our only chance, we must get him back to the other side. Jackson, we need your sisters here. The only way we can defeat him is to forgive jack. Daddy wanted everyone Jack ever loved to hate him. Your sisters and mother, even my sisters and brothers. The only way is to be forgiven purely."

Lorraine said.

Jack begin to fade and transform from boy to a man. Jackson watched as his father begin to look exactly the way he did when he abused him as a child.

"He knows you are here, he wants you to see Jack the way you used to remember. Jackson, you must let the past go. Your father didn't harm you, he was being controlled by my evil father."

Lorraine said.

Jackson wanted to believe that but the fact remained he was seeing the man he hated."

"Jackson, son I never meant you any harm."

His father said.

Jackson didn't say a word instead he looked him square in the eyes.

"Why should I help you after all the things you did to us?" Jackson said through clenched teeth.

"Son I never tried to hurt you. I love you and your sisters but what was inside of me. The thing that lived in me I had no control of. The days I fought it were all of the good days we had. As he got stronger I became weaker. Son you have to know that I would never intentionally harm you. I wrote those letters to show you that I was fighting this...this...thing. The day I thought I saw Pauline it was really him. He pushed me down those steps and I seen him. I tried saving that young boy but he turned me to a child."

Jack said.

"You see Jackson this thing has been behind all of this. We can't stop it until Jack crosses over."

Lorraine said.

Jackson remembered how messed up his marriage was. Just maybe this could help him clear his own demons.

"Okay let's do this."

Jackson said.

Jackson could hear the faint knocking again.

"Someone is here from the other side, quick you have to get back. We can distract him, tell your sisters I love them."

Jack said before opening the closet door.

Jackson eased out of the closet with Lorraine closely behind him.

"I will see you when you get back son."

Jack said giving him one final look.

He opened the bedroom door and walked towards the back bedroom, down the hallway. Lorraine quickly shut the bedroom door after Jack. The loud footsteps shook the house as it ran past the room. Lorraine waited a moment then opened the door.

"Hurry, go back get the others Jackson!"

She said rushing him towards the living room.

Jackson saw his body laying there, and laid down exactly the same way. He woke up to someone knocking at the door. Feeling throbbing pain in the back of his head he quickly opened the front door.

"Jackson I been calling you all day. You haven't checked your messages?"

Joy asked him.

Jackson looked around and stepped outside. Walking to Joy's car he touched it and felt that it was real.

"Jackson what the hell is wrong with you?" Joy spat.

"Get in the car let's go!"

Jackson said getting in the passenger side.

Joy got in her car and drove to no particular destination.

"Jackson! Are you going to tell me what's up with you?"

Joy asked.

"I gotta get the fuck away from around here. This some Freddy Kruger paranormal mixed with exorcist type shit."

Jackson said wanting a drink.

Feeling the back of his head, he felt dampness and saw that it was blood.

"See now this shit for the birds."

Jackson said.

"Will you please tell me what happened to your head?"

Joy asked.

"If I tell you what I just seen you literally would not believe me."

Jackson said.

"Now, I got to here this because you're acting really weird."

Joy said.

"Joy, I just got done talking to daddy's soul and his sister Lorraine."

Jackson said.

"What? Jackson, aunt Lorraine died before we were born."

Joy said confused.

"Joy I'm telling you this shit is real I woke up dead and saw everything."

Jackson told her.

"Jackson, how in the hell do you wake up dead?"

Joy laughed.

"See you laughing but I'm dead ass serious."

Jackson said.

"Okay wait a minute, start from the beginning were you drinking again tonight?"

Joy asked.

"No I was not for your information Joy!"

Jackson said.

"My bad, I had to make sure go head."

Joy said.

"I went to therapy and she suggested that I reach out to daddy. Work out our issues or whatever so I can move on. I went to the house lit some candles and started talking just like I am now. I remember saying daddy if you're in this house show me a sign. Next thing I know something grabs me by my ankle. I ended up hitting my head on the floor and was knocked. Then I saw myself laying there on the floor. Like an out of body type thing, that's why I thought I was dead. Then I saw a little boy but it was daddy as child. He told me to hide from this beast. It had fiery eyes, looked like something off a horror movie. So, he tells me he wants me to see how this all started. I held his hand and sort of traveled back in time. Daddy's father wasn't his father. Grandma must have stepped out on him. Cause once he found out daddy wasn't his, he treated him like shit, beat on him, humiliated him. It wasn't until, when aunt Lorraine was raped and killed that the curse started. Daddy ran to go get help but when he reached home it was too late. After that he vowed to make daddy feel his pain when he had children of his own. I think daddy messed up when he killed him years later. Right after his mother passed, he killed that man. His spirit haunted daddy and that's who made him do all them fucked up things to us."

Jackson told her.

"Let me get this straight you saying daddy killed his stepfather. Which caused him to treat us like shit. All because he was haunted by his stepfather. Who blamed him for aunt Lorraine's death.'

Joy said.

"I know it sounds unbelievable but I saw it."

Jackson said.

"At first, I thought maybe Carmen and the kids leaving has taken a toll on you. Now I think you really just need to go somewhere and get you some professional help Jackson. We all been through a lot this year." Joy spoke.

"I'm not crazy Joy and for once could you hear me out?"

Jackson spat.

"Jasmine lost the baby today and we were trying to reach you. David flipped out, killed an officer. Then shot himself in front her. So, forgive me for caring about our baby sister Jackson."

Joy said.

"Damn, if it's not one thing it's another."

Jackson said.

"Look, I need you and Jasmine's help with this. I know now ain't the time but the sooner the better."

Jackson said.

"You're my brother and I love you dearly but."

Joy said shaking her head.

"Come on Joy you know me well enough to know when I'm being serious."

Jackson said.

"Okay I believe you are serious. What exactly do you need me and Jas for?"

Joy asked.

"Daddy needs forgiveness and I know you already forgave him. I haven't and apparently neither has Jasmine. We have to do this together as a family."

Jackson said.

"Okay when Jasmine heals up, I will try to explain all of that. Jackson, this is a onetime thing after this no more."

Joy warned.

"That's fine with me this shit got me wanting a blunt."

Jackson laughed.

"Until then you should stay at my place. Can't have you in that house unconscious."

Joy said.

"I gotta make things right with my wife and kids. I don't want to die and later on need their forgiveness to cross over."

Jackson said.

"You will fix that situation because you are better than that."

Joy said and smiled at him.

Driving to her house, Jackson was relieved he was spending time with the living. Jasmine was in a bit of a daze as she laid on the couch.

"Hey baby sis! How you holding up?"

Jackson asked her. "

I'm okay I guess, just feeling a little down."

She replied.

"That's understandable it ain't going to go away overnight. Give it time sis, we all here for you."

Jackson told her.

The three sat in silence, each deep in thought. This year was rough and each battled with personal issues. Jackson missed his family who was miles away. Jasmine lost her entire family and was all alone. Joy embraced motherhood but secretly fears she will fail her child.

Then there was the fact that Jack had left this world leaving a bad taste in everyone's lives. All they had were one another and right now each could use a shoulder. Jackson laughed to himself as he remembered a saying of his mother's came to mind. Who used to tell them whenever you're sad just remember a knock, knock joke.

"Knock knock." Jackson said.

"Whose there?"

Joy asked out loud.

"Hung."

Jackson replied.

"Hung who?"

Jasmine asked.

"Hung-ree now what y'all cook?"

Jackson asked.

The three off them laughed and remember how their mother used to cheer them up.

"I guess momma was right knock, knock jokes do make you feel better."

Jasmine said.

"No matter what, we gone always have each other's back." Jackson said.

"I guess we stuck together."

Joy added with a smile.

For the next few days the siblings stood behind Jasmine while she grieved. David's family reached out to her. His parents mainly, came over and spoke to Jasmine.

"Are there any insurance policies you had on my David?"

His mother asked her.

"Yes we had insurance on one another."

Jasmine replied.

"Surely there must be something in writing to show he was married not even three months. Most policies require you to be married for a certain amount of time. Or did you get a policy that accepts thirty days to collect."

She asked.

"Are you trying to say my sister had something to do with David's death!"

Joy spat.

"I got this Joy, look I didn't look into the insurance policies that close. David picked them, I don't want anything. You can have the damn policy and house too. I don't need anything of your son's. He and I weren't even together. Did he tell you that I walked in on him having sex with another man? Before all of this happened that is what this was about. I planned on leaving him and he couldn't accept that. Or maybe he didn't want anyone to know. I lost our child due to all of this, did you know that?"

Jasmine cried.

"I had no idea, my David wouldn't do such a thing. If anyone is to blame, it's you! He was fine until he married you. I told him he should hold off but he insisted that he wanted you. If I find out you are the cause of my David killing himself, I will take you for every worthless penny you have!"

She spat.

"Vivian!" David's father said upset that she said those harsh words.

"I think its best that you leave. On second thought let me tell you one thing Vivian. I worked hard for every penny I got. Might not come from wealth but my father raised me to work hard. I owned my own shop, before I was with your son. I had my own money so don't sit up here and act like I was only after some money. I just lost my first child, on top of that recently had to bury my father. You think I give a damn about some insurance money. Tell you what, take my name off of everything. The policy, the house, hell, you can have it all. Here's the ring too there's nothing else of your son tied to me. You go your way and I will go mine. Now would you be so kind to get the fuck out of here!"

Jasmine spat slamming her ring down on the table.

Vivian quickly took the ring and hurried to the front door.

"I apologize for all of this Jasmine. None of this is your fault we are not hurting for anything. You keep what you had with my son. I will deal with her don't worry about a thing."

David's father replied.

Joy saw them to the door as they left. Jackson paced back and forth in the kitchen.

"That woman has lost her damn mind! She has no right implying that you had anything to do with their fucked up son killing himself."

Jackson fumed.

"You got that right I wanted to slap the taste out of her mouth."

Joy spat.

"What if this is all my fault? Maybe if I had of talked to him it wouldn't have ended like this."

Jasmine cried.

"Jas this isn't your fault okay. David did what he did all on his own. Don't go blaming yourself over something you had no control over. We got your back no matter what. So forget about what his bitter ass mother had to say. We know the truth we know you did nothing except love him. You don't owe no explanation for that."

Jackson told her.

"That's exactly how I see it too. you didn't do a damn thing wrong little sister."

Joy said as she embraced her.

Jackson hugged them both as Jasmine cried on their shoulders. This was a lot on her emotionally. She hadn't even grieved yet and already had to deal with David's messy mother. Only God knows what will happen once they lay him to rest. Whatever happens, Jasmine had no worries. At least she had her big brother and sister to have her back.

Chapter Eleven

Joy, Jasmine, Jackson

"When Three Touch and Agree"

"Follow me please."

The usher said as Jasmine stepped into the Cathedral. Joy and Jackson were right behind her along with Juniqua and Elijah. They were all attending David's funeral in attempt to support Jasmine. The church was filled with his friends, family and colleagues. The usher lead them to sit on the opposite side of David's family.

Joy was so furious of the way they were treating Jasmine. Placing them all near the back like she wasn't his wife. David's parents sat up front along with some other woman.

"Jasmine we can leave whenever you want. This is ridiculous how that woman is treating you."

Joy said in a low tone, careful not to speak too loud out of respect. Jasmine simply took a seat and didn't utter a word. She wanted to pay her respects and leave. She signed the house over to David's mother.

The insurance from his policy went towards his funeral. His mother made sure to pick out the most expensive casket that the insurance could cover. Leaving nothing to Jasmine but the money in the bank account.

Vivian even had the bank to track each and every deposit David ever made. That way only his money could go directly to her. Through it all Jasmine didn't say a word. Had it been up to Joy she would have told Vivian exactly where she could go and what she could kiss.

The service began and the directors passed out the obituary. Reading David's obituary Joy saw that Jasmine wasn't even mentioned.

"Oh hell no Jas you're not even on here.""

Joy whispered.

"It's okay Joy she can do as she pleases."

Jasmine said sadly.

Joy wanted to make a scene but out of respect of her sister she didn't. Vivian was called up to say a few words and things really got bad.

"My son was always brave and driven."

Vivian said as she paused briefly to add emotional effect.

"And also gay."

Joy mumbled still pissed about Jasmine not being in her husband's obituary.

"He was going through so much. Sometimes as parents you don't understand why your children choose to be around the wrong individuals. I should have done more to have kept that person from around him. To all the parents I just want to say protect you kids. Even as they grow they still make mistakes. We can see what they don't and prevent situations like this from happening. My son's very special friend would like to share a few words. She's more like a daughter-in-law to me please come Leslie."

Vivian smiled as the woman who had sat up front stood. That's where Jasmine should have sat. David told Jasmine all about Leslie. She knew he and Leslie dated throughout college. This was the up most disrespectful thing Vivian could do. Like a slap in the face Jasmine simply placed her head down.

"I loved David very much and he loved me as well. We lost touch because of an old friend of his. He was supposed to be the one I eventually walked down the aisle with."

The woman said.

That was the last straw Jasmine couldn't take anymore. Standing up she was ready to go. Jackson sat at the end and saw that everyone on the pew they sat on was standing. He stood and stepped aside as Jasmine scooted pass. Tears ran down her cheek as she tried to reach the exit. The usher blocked the exit and tried to get them to sit down.

"Since you all want a scene then fuck it let's do it!"

Jasmine spat.

Walking up the aisle she kicked off her heels. The look on Vivian's face was priceless.

"Oh don't you dare look at me like I'm crazy because you ain't seen crazy yet!"

Jasmine yelled.

Grabbing the organ player's microphone, she stood in front of David's casket.

"I am David's wife, well was soon to be ex-wife. I loved every inch of this fucker. When my father died do you know what he was doing? Any of you want to guess what perfect David was doing?"

Jasmine yelled into the mic.

Joy and Jackson walked up the aisle to get Jasmine.

"He was fucking that man right there! Yeah him right, right there third row in the peach button up. Hell, they sat you up closer than me and I'm his wife. Don't act shy now, I know you remember me. I'm the chick that interrupted you two fucking in a Days Inn motel room in the shower. On the day of my father's funeral! Does that refresh your memory Mr. Booty bandit."

Jasmine said.

The man stood and the woman beside him jumped up.

"Charles, is that true? Were you and David messing around?"

She yelled.

The whole congregation was waiting on Charles to answer. He looked at Jasmine and she dared him to tell a lie in the house of the Lord.

"Veronica, I can explain it was only one time. David had said no one will find out, he had done it before."

Charles said.

Veronica slapped him and the congregation starting whispering. A few of them pulled out their phones.

"You told me that you were frat brothers. He's been in our home, he's been around our kids, how could you?"

She cried.

Charles couldn't even look at her, instead he left like a coward.

"The truth hurts sometimes and I didn't want to believe it either Veronica. I rather a man tell me the ugly truth, then a pretty lie."

Jasmine said and a few people nodded in agreement.

"How dare you ruin my son's service with this drama!"

Vivian spat.

Jasmine turned around towards the pulpit where both her and David's ex stood standing there. Looking at her as if she was crazy.

"Oh you miserable, uppity, disrespectful, conniving bitch!

You have the audacity to invite his ex-girlfriend. Knowing that I'm married to your very gay cynical son. Sit her up here, you didn't even mention me on his obituary. I have been quiet, I let you dictate his funeral you got every penny your son made, even the house we bought. But you will not disrespect me anymore! I came here for closure because I will move on. I'm not going to let what your son did to me hinder me from being the woman I worked hard to become. So, fuck you and that knock off wannabe Stacy Dash looking bitch. He wasn't too brave if he couldn't be himself and come out so, I'm coming out for him."

Jasmine spat before dropping the mic.

The congregation gasped at Jasmine's bluntness.

"LGBT power y'all!"

Joy said pumping her fist in the air as she walked towards the exit after her sister.

Jackson let the kids ride with him. Jasmine laughed hysterically once she got in the car with Joy. Looking at her sister sideways Joy wanted to know what was so funny.

"Um Jas, are you feeling alright?"

Joy asked.

"I just crashed my own husband's funeral. I wouldn't be surprised if somebody recorded me."

Jasmine laughed.

"You did tear that funeral the hell up."

Joy laughed.

"I feel better now that everything is out."

Jasmine said.

"Good sis, we both going to look back on this one day."

Joy said smiling.

"And have one hell of a story to tell our grandkids."

Jasmine replied.

"I love you girl and I got you till the world blow up."

Joy said hugging Jasmine.

"And I love you too."

Jasmine said in tears.

"See you gone have me crying cause you crying."

Joy said as she wiped her eyes.

"Sorry I can't help it."

Jasmine laughed.

"Fuck now I'm tearing up."

Joy said as a tear slid down her cheek.

"You ready to do this?"

Jasmine asked.

"As ready as I'm gone be."

Joy sighed.

They rode to the old house while Jackson dropped Elijah and Juniqua over Nathan's place.

"So this is the house daddy grew up in, its big."

Joy said as she parked.

"Yeah I wonder why daddy never brought us out here."

Jasmine said looking around.

Their uncle Walter agreed to let them tour the house alone for a few hours. Jackson pulled up just as Jasmine and Joy was getting out the car.

"Y'all this is what I was telling you about.'

Jackson said getting out his truck.

"Alright let's go."

Joy said walking up the steps.

Once the three were on the porch the rocking chair begin to rock slowly.

"Aw hell no y'all see that?"

Jasmine said.

"Jas calm down, yo scary self that ain't nothing but the wind. Jackson, you got the keys to unlock the door, so we can get this over with?"

Joy said.

Jackson placed the key in the door and unlocked it. Pushing the door open, the door let out a loud creak as he pushed it open. Jackson was the first to step inside of the house.

"If this was a movie I would be telling us to turn around and get the fuck away from here."

Jasmine said.

"There's nothing to be afraid of Jas you watch too many scary movies."

Joy replied.

Jackson walked around the coffee table and saw the old man with red eyes out of his peripheral.

"Uh y'all mind coming over on this side of the room."

Jackson said trying not to alarm his sisters.

Jasmine shut the door and stepped towards Jackson.

"Why we got to be on this side of the, oh my damn."

Jasmine said hitting the mannequin challenge.

She didn't move or blink once she saw what Jackson was seeing.

"What now Jas you overreacting."

Joy said getting upset.

"Um Joy no she's not."

Jackson tried to tell Joy but the man began to walk behind Joy.

"No Jackson don't take her side she been flapping about this and that since we walked in here."

Joy said.

"Joy if you know well enough you would hit the mannequin and shut the hell up."

Jasmine said standing stiff.

Joy noticed Jackson wasn't moving either.

"Why do I need to be quiet for?"

Joy went on as she felt a cool breeze on the back of her neck. Looking out of her peripheral she continued to talk and saw that something or someone was behind her.

"See that's the problem we all here for what?"

Joy said walking towards Jackson.

The man was still standing where Joy was standing. Joy kept going on and on while slightly turning and looking out of the corner of her eye over her shoulder. Her heart raced as she too saw it.

"Joy did you catch..."

Jas tried asking her sister if she saw the man but Joy cut her off.

"Ain't shit to catch you hear me not nothing.

Now Jackson show me where the bathroom is."

Joy said.

Jackson turned on the hallway light and the man ran down the hall. Jasmine hauled ass out the front door and Joy didn't short stop.

"Unlock the door Joy!"

Jasmine yelled running to the car.

"Jackson bring yo ass the fuck on!"

Joy hollered.

They hopped in the car and Joy started up the car. Hitting a U-turn she watched as Jackson ran to his truck.

"Go! Go! Go! He on the porch, he on the porch. Lord please let us live and make it out of here alive."

Jasmine yelled jumping up and down in her seat. Jackson started up his truck and Joy sped off. Looking in her review mirror she watched as her brother did a U-turn and sped behind her. Joy drove to her house and Jackson pulled up behind her. He was the first to break the silence.

"I told y'all this shit was real."

Jackson said.

"Man, he can have that house, daddy dead he will be just fine. I'm not fucking with them ghost."

Joy said.

"What you say, damn that let the dead be dead."

Jasmine said.

"I need y'all on this, we need to go to daddy house, and help him cross over, so this shit can be over with."

Jackson said.

"Who do what? Shit if daddy want a crossover he better hit up Allen Iverson. That's the crossover king."

Jasmine said.

"Jackson, we believe you now but as far as dealing with them ghosts count me out."

Joy said.

"That's the only way we can end it."

He told her.

"After all daddy did to y'all, why should we help?"

Jasmine said.

"It's hard to explain but you have to see the truth for yourself."

Jackson said.

"Look as long as we don't have to go back to our grandparent's

home I'm cool."

Jasmine said.

"This is our last field trip Jackson."

Joy said.

"All I need is one chance."

Jackson replied with a smile.

They headed over to their parent's house. Jackson lit candles just like last time.

"This the same shit them white folks did on exorcist. It ain't no Priest and everybody didn't make it. So I'm gone say this once every man for themselves."

Jasmine said.

"I'll remember that if you trip or fall."

Joy spat rolling her eyes at her.

"I know how to roll over and keep going."

Jasmine said.

"Okay the last time I did this I was knocked out. So, I figured we should lay on our backs and try falling asleep. Let me know when you both ready."

Jackson said getting on the floor.

"Oh hell no, I just got my hair done this floor dirty as hell."

Joy spat.

"Suit yourself, I guess you prefer being knocked out."

Jackson said.

"You don't gotta tell me twice."

Jasmine said laying next to Jackson.

Joy laid beside Jasmine and the three was so close you would of thought they were glued to one another.

"Damn Jas, I shouldn't be close enough to hear your heartbeat." Jackson said.

"Well Joy cutting off my circulation to my arm and you don't hear me complaining. We in this together if one die the other gotta die. I will live on for you both."

Jasmine said.

"You mean if one die we all die."

Joy said.

"Hell naw, somebody gotta live to tell it."

Jasmine replied.

"I guess that somebody has to be you huh."

Jackson said.

"Well since you insist I guess so," she said.

"Jackson this isn't working and I'm not tired enough to go to sleep."

Joy said.

"Okay let me just think, maybe if I try talking to them someone will come."

Jackson said.

"Say what! I thought you said we was helping daddy and that's it?"

Jasmine said.

"Jas will you shut up"

I hope it get yo ass first."

Joy spat.

"If it get me when I die I'm gone come back and get you. We just gone be some getting motherfuckers."

Jasmine said.

Tired of his sisters acting like children, Jackson decided to get this over with.

"Aunt Lorraine! It's us we're here now."

Jackson said.

"See I knew I should have stayed in the car."

Joy said.

The floorboards shook and the three of them held hands.

"Lord please don't let us be killed."

Jasmine said.

A loud crash from the kitchen and made them jump.

"It must be the monster that heard us, we gotta go somewhere else."

Jackson whispered getting up.

They all headed to Joy's old bedroom. Stepping into the closet, Jackson told them to get in. Jasmine shut the bedroom door then got in the closet with them. She shut the door and the shelf above them fell. Causing them to fall and black out.

Jackson opened his eyes, looking down at his body. He waited to see if Joy and Jasmine had crossed over.

You came back I'm glad to see you."

Lorraine said to Jackson.

He hugged her and both Joy along with Jasmine appeared in spirit form.

"This is some ex-files type of shit."

Joy said.

"You look so much like your mother."

Lorraine smiled.

"Joy and Jas this aunt Lorraine."

Jackson smiled.

"Oh wow aunt Lorraine."

Jasmine said hugging her.

Joy was next to hug her.

"Your father has gotten lost we must find him."

Lorraine said.

"Aunt Lorraine can you show them what dad showed me?"
Jackson said.

"Okay but we must hurry, quick Joy and Jasmine each place one of your hands into mine," she said.

Jackson kept watch as they traveled into the past. Music started to play from afar. Unsure of whether he should leave or not. Jackson hid underneath the bed. When the bedroom door opened, Jackson saw the foot of the demon.

He opened the closet door then shut it. Jackson was grateful that they were all gone, and that this being, could not see beyond this world of the un-living.

Running out of the room it left and Jackson was relieved and got up from under the bed. When they all were back, both Joy and Jasmine were shocked.

"You were right Jackson we seen everything."

Jasmine said.

"How long has the music been playing Jackson?"

Lorraine asked.

"Right after you all left."

He replied.

"There's another soul here, did someone die from the other side?" She asked.

"My husband killed himself but other than that no."

Jasmine said.

"It wasn't an accident he's using your husband to get to us."
Lorraine said.

"He who?"
Joy asked.

"My father."
Lorraine said as she peeped out of the bedroom doorway.
They all followed her down the hall.

"This looks just like the house but different."
Jasmine whispered.

"This may seem like the other side but it is very different.
Jack must be at our old house."
Lorraine said.

"The house we went to the first time with the creepy old
man. Oh, no, no, no we can't go back there."
Jasmine said.

"It's the only way."
Lorraine said.

"Fine let's get daddy and just get out of there."
Jasmine replied.

Lorraine led them down a dark path that ended at a big
brown door.

"Whatever you do, stay together. He will try to use horrible
memories to turn you against your father. Don't fall apart you
have to fight through the bad memories."
Lorraine said.

"Won't you be with us?"
Joy asked.

"If I go past this door I can't come back. So, you three have
to do it alone. This is as far as I can go but I will be here waiting
for you." She said.

Jackson opened the door and was the first to walk through.

Chapter Twelve

Joy, Jasmine, Jackson

"Forgiving Our Father"

As the door closed behind Jackson, he tried to pry it open to get to his sisters.

"Jasmine! Joy! Open the door it's not working."

Jackson called out while pounding on the door.

Jackson looked around and heard arguing. Following the voices, he saw his father and mother. Jack hauled off and slapped her.

"Nooo!"

Jackson yelled trying to fight his father.

Remembering what Lorraine said this was just bad memories. Trying to ignore his mother's cries Jackson walked away. Only to walk into another bad memory. This time Jackson's father was drowning his mother in the bathtub. Tears ran down his face as Jackson watched his mother fight to breathe.

He couldn't take much more. The more the memories came, the more he started hating Jack all over again. Jackson finally made it to a red door. He heard the music playing from the other side of the door.

Dionne Warwick's "Walk On Bye" was playing over and over. Jackson heard screams and knew they were his mother's. Placing his hands over his ears he tried to ignore the screams.

Joy and Jasmine stepped through the door searching for Jackson.

"I don't like this Joy its dark in here."

Jasmine said as they were sure to stay close together. Hearing a squeaking sound, they both followed the sound. Opening another door, they walked into what was Joy's old room.

Joy saw herself as a young girl and Jack on top of her. Froze, she begin to cry seeing her past right in front of her. This was the Jack she remembered.

"Oh my god."

Jasmine said covering her mouth. She couldn't believe that was her father doing that to her own sister. Grabbing Joy's hand, they left the room and walked into another painful memory.

"Either you going to do it or I will go get Jasmine to come do it!"

Jack said as he pulled his pants down. Joy saw herself as a child again forced to do the unthinkable. Getting on her knees she did exactly as Jack told her. Joy stood trembling each memory was slowly breaking her down.

"Joy let's keep going we don't have to watch that. Remember it's trying to trick us."

Jasmine said.

It still didn't help that Joy went through all of that. They kept going until they were at Elijah's being born. Joy began to cry as she saw them hand her son to the couple that paid her father. Jack didn't deserve her help after all he put her through.

"I can't do this Jasmine. You didn't have to go through what I had to. This is too much, even if he was possessed it still was my father."

Joy cried.

"I know and you went through it because you were protecting me. Joy let's put this behind us once and for all."

Jasmine cried.

Joy wiped her tears and went on. Jasmine saw the day David killed himself. Joy took a closer look and saw that the old man was behind David.

"Jasmine look!"

Joy said showing her that it wasn't David that killed himself.

'The old man did this to us."

Jasmine said.

"Like you said we have to stop this."

Joy said.

Looking up ahead they saw Jackson covering his ears.

"There's Jackson come on."

Joy said running towards him.

Jasmine went right behind her the three embraced.

"This memory shit ain't no joke." Jackson said.

"Who you telling?! It took everything in me not to breakdown."

Joy said.

"The music is coming from behind this door."

Jasmine said.

"Jack must be in there, you ready for this Joy?" Jackson said.

"I think so."

She replied and the door opened.

Walking through the door they were back inside of Lorraine and Jack's parent's house. The walls shook and there were screams. Jackson held his sisters' hands and quickly went into a bedroom.

"Let's go through this window."

Jackson said.

Putting them through the window first. The bedroom door was kicked open. Jackson jumped out of the window.

"Run! Go! Go!"

He yelled getting up from the ground as the beast showed its ugly head through the window. With red eyes and a head of horns. It was black as tar and hands had long sharp fingernails. This had definitely come straight from Hell itself.

Running around the back of the house, Jack was beside the creek. Joy stopped dead in her tracks. He looked exactly like he had when he used to molest her.

"Joy come on!"

Jasmine said grabbing her hand. Jack saw how Joy hesitated and knew it was because of the things he had done.

"Joy you look so different all grown up." He smiled.

"Daddy we all been through a lot to get here. Especially Joy and Jackson with the bad memories."

Jasmine said.

"I'm sorry, and I know that's not good enough but I would have never done anything to hurt you all." He said.

"Why didn't you fight to stop it then!'

Joy spat filled with rage.

"I tried, you seen how strong he is. He even made me think I could do something like that on my own."

Jack teared up.

"Why should we believe you. For all we know you were doing this all on your own." Joy said.

"Joy I know I hurt you the most but it wasn't me. It was what was inside of me and I'm finally rid of him. If I knew the only way to get rid of him was to die. I would have killed myself years ago. It kept me bound for years, and I finally fought it long enough. That's when I wrote those letters and tried to reach you."

Jack said.

"All this time and now you wanna fight it."

Joy said.

"I'm the real Jack, the one you barely got to know. I never gave up fighting Joy or else you wouldn't be here." He smiled.

"I only remember the bad, there wasn't any good." Joy said.

"I can take all the bad away all you have to do is forgive me."

He said.

"I don't know if I can do that." Joy said.

"Of course she can't, Jasmine couldn't forgive me!"

David said from behind them.

"What do you want?" Jack asked.

"Come on Jackie you and I both know what he wants."

David smiled.

"I will never give my soul to that demon just because he did." Jack said.

"He who?" Jackson asked.

"The old man," Jack referred to his mother's husband.

David grabbed Jasmine, both Jack and Jackson fought him. Joy took her sister's hand while they fought him off. Running through the creek hands began to pull at their legs and feet. Fighting them off, they tried to make it across.

Jackson ran to help them and Jack told them to keep going and he will meet them. They made it back to the door. Lorraine held it open for them. Joy and Jasmine were the first to reach her. Jackson saw Jack behind him being chased by the demon.

"Hurry we must go! He can cross this door!"

Lorraine said.

Jasmine and Joy ran ahead just as Jackson made it through the door. He followed Lorraine and nearly fell as the ground shook. Jack closed the door behind him, to buy some time. Joy and jasmine was back in the room where they fell in the closet.

"We can't cross over until Jack is loved and forgiven from all who he hurt"

Lorraine said.

Jack ran into the room and placed the bed in front of the door. The walls shook and they were running out of time.

"I forgive you daddy."

Jasmine said hugging him.

"I forgive you too."

Jackson said hugging him.

Joy was the last step to him.

"The past is the past so, I forgive you too." She said.

Jack hugged Joy and he took those memories away from her. Jack began to fade and so did Lorraine.

"Go back to the other side and remember we will always be with you."

She told them before completely disappearing.

"I love you all."

Jack said looking at the three of them as if he were seeing them for the first time."

Jackson rushed them into the closet so that they could go. Moments later, they each was waking up. Jackson pulled the shelf off of them. Joy helped Jasmine up and they left the closet. Jackson shut the closet door ready to get out of the house.

"Let's go because that was too much to go through all over again."

Jasmine said.

The three left and headed outside to the car.

"I'm glad all of this is finally done."

Joy said.

"I am cool on doing that shit again."

Jackson laughed.

This time Jackson saw his father smiling and waving dressed in white. He looked at peace and so did aunt Lorraine. He could now move on with his life. The first thing he was going to do was go see his kids.

Sneak Peek

What Happens In This House 3

"Facing Demons"

Jack has crossed over and things are beginning to look up for all three siblings. Joy has decided to coach the girls at Canto High. Just when things were getting normal, life throws her another curve.

Jasmine has been having the time of her life with a certain someone in her life. The two have gotten extremely close and has no plans on slowing down.

Elijah has another addition to his already big problem. Balancing ball, school and both baby mommas his hands are full.

Jackson has a new woman in his life and has come to terms that his marriage is over. The moment he decides to move on tragedy strikes and causes him and Carmen to come to terms that they might still need one another.

This time the trio doesn't have to come to the house. Instead, each is paid a house visit and there's only one way to stop it and that's by sticking together.

Elijah was laid back on his bed as Jacquees' "bounce" played. Riley winded her body to the beat. While the thick clouds of smoke released from her lips. Climbing on top of him she passed him the blunt.

"Gone head and take that shit off girl."

He said inhaling the smoke.

Riley turned around reverse cowgirl and made her ass bounce. Lifting up her hoody, she tossed it on the floor. Next, she pulled her tank top over her head. Her bra and boy shorts was the only remaining clothes.

Pulling out his phone Elijah recorded Riley's ass twerking on his snapchat. Slapping her on her ass he was hard and ready to get explicit. Pulling her beside him in bed he tugged at her shorts.

"You trying to make that ass bounce on me?"

He asked her.

"If you can handle it."

She teased.

"Girl you know I can handle anything."

He smiled.

"Elijah which one did you like the…"

Juniqua asked walking in but was shocked that he had company.

"Wow so this is what you're doing while everyone else is at work. Then on top of that yo dumbass got this thot in ya mother's house."

Juniqua spat.

"Thot! bitch I know you're not calling me no thot. Elijah check that homeless whore or else I will."

Riley said yelling.

"Really Elijah, so you sitting around dogging me to the next bitch. You two are perfect for each other. Make one hell of a lesbian couple."

Juniqua said.

Riley jumped up and Elijah had to separate them.

"Riley chill! That's my child she's carrying, now both of you chill."

Elijah yelled.

"She's not the only one carrying your child!"

Riley spat.

"Say what!"

Elijah said shocked.

"When were you going to tell me?"

He asked her.

"Doesn't matter now, you know? Besides, how do you know the bastard she's carrying is even yours? Ya girl is well known over in Jackson from what I here."

Riley said with a smirk.

"Bitch I will beat the fuck out of ya!"

Juniqua tried to run past Elijah to get to her...

TO BE CONTINUED!

Have You Read More books by Aleia Latay?
What Happens In This House 3
Definition Of A Real Man
All The Things Your Man Won't Do
For the Holidays
Count It Up

True Glory Publications
IF YOU WOULD LIKE TO BE A PART OF OUR TEAM,
PLEASE SEND YOUR SUBMISSIONS BY EMAIL TO
TRUEGLORYPUBLICATIONS@GMAIL.COM.
PLEASE INCLUDE A BRIEF BIO, A SYNOPSIS OF
THE BOOK, AND THE FIRST THREE CHAPTERS.
SUBMIT USING MICROSOFT WORD WITH FONT IN
11 TIMES NEW ROMAN.